BEBE and BEN

BEBE and BEN

JILL ALLGOOD

ROBERT HALE & COMPANY

ISBN 0 7091 4942 5

Robert Hale & Company
Clerkenwell House
Clerkenwell Green
London EC1 0HT

Composed by Specialised Offset Services Ltd, Liverpool
and printed and bound in Great Britain by
Redwood Burn Limited Trowbridge and Esher

CONTENTS

ILLUSTRATIONS

To
PHILIP AND JOE

ACKNOWLEDGEMENTS

My sincere thanks and appreciation to: Eamonn Andrews and Thames Television; Fred Astaire; Bob Block; The British Broadcasting Corporation; Barbara Lyon Burkitt and Colin Burkitt; Actor Cordell Jnr and *The Atlanta Journal and Constitution Magazine*; Lily Coyle; Joan Crawford; Brenda Davies and The British Film Institute; Ken Dodd; Anne Edwards of the *Sunday Express*; Father Carmine de Felici; Florence Foster; Daphne Frizell; Her Serene Highness Princess Grace de Monaco; Margot Grahame; Joyce Grenfell; Thelma Holland; Frankie Howerd; Muriel Hughes; Eileen Hunter; Jean Hutton; Paul Irwin and *The Rand Daily Mail*, Johannesburg, South Africa; Glenda Jackson; Margaret Lockwood; Arthur Lowe; Angela and Richard Lyon; Cecil Madden, M.B.E., F.R.S.A.; The Executors of the André Maurois Estate, Jonathan Cape Ltd and the translator, Gerard Hopkins, for quotations from *The Life of Sir Alexander Fleming*; Sonia, Lady Melchett; The Rev. Dewi D. Morgan; The National Film Archive; Dame Anna Neagle, D.B.E.; Perlita Neilson; Natalie Oliver; The Editor, *Radio Times*; The Radio Times Hulton Picture Library; Ethel Revnell; Doris Rogers; Anthony Slide, Editor, *The Silent Picture*; Virginia Graham Thesiger; Max Wall; Molly Weir; Herbert Wilcox, O.B.E.; The Honourable John Hay Whitney (formerly His Excellency The American Ambassador in London); Edward Woodward.

And my personal thanks are also due to: Philip and Joe; George Davey; John Elmer; Maureen and Suzanne; Stephen Mason; Reginal Keates; Trevor Nicholas; Dennis Young and the folk of Panad.

*My admiration for Bebe and Ben was intense —
shared, I believe, with millions of British
people. They were a tonic and a cocktail.*

Herbert Wilcox

PREFACE

One outstanding quality of vivid personalities is the gift of making lasting impressions on people and events. When Bebe Daniels married Ben Lyon in Hollywood and the Press quipped 'Daniels In The Lyon's Den', they were not aware then that Bebe and Ben would leave indelible impressions on people and events that the years would never erase.

In the years before the Lyon captured his Daniels, their lives in some ways were exact opposites; in others, almost identical. Bebe was born into the theatre, and knew the loneliness of being an only child in a world of adults. Ben was born into home life; he had two sisters and a brother. His schooldays were consistent. As a child actress, Bebe's schooldays were often inconsistent. In her early teens Bebe became a star of silent pictures. Ben was seventeen when he got his first stage break in a play called *Seventeen*. At the time Ben was in New York. Bebe was 3,000 miles away in Hollywood, California. But they both travelled in theatre stock companies, Bebe as a child, Ben as a young man. Then he broke into films and went to Hollywood. After several years of separate careers in the theatre and films they met and finally married. As international stars their husband and wife partnership lasted nearly forty-one years. They became rich and famous; they had setbacks and disasters; they made money and lost money. Paradoxically, while outwardly they were independent and self-assured, there was often the need for reassurance and dependence on others. They formed unshakeable friendships. They were generous and their generosity was matched by a warmth and depth of character which endeared them to millions. They were equally at home with kings and commoners. And they created an ideal marriage which became a legend.

No scandal touched their names, except once. During the war when Ben, in the U.S. Eighth Army Air Force, was in Washington on a special assignment, he went to California. Bebe was in London. The late Hedda Hopper, rival Hollywood columnist to Louella Parsons their great friend, wrote an unfounded and unwarranted report that a divorce between Bebe and Ben was "imminent". This was the only time divorce was associated with their names. Ben took swift retaliatory action. Hedda Hopper never mentioned them again in her column.

Bebe Daniels and Ben Lyon were born in a momentous year – 1901. The twentieth century had arrived. Charles Lamb once wrote: "No one ever regarded the first of January with indifference." Certainly no one regarded with indifference the pealing of bells as they heralded in the first of January 1901. Reluctantly, the old century gave way to the new with the end of a great era. Queen Victoria was soon to die and the Edwardian era to be born. It was a time for innovation and of invention. Scientists and engineers were casting long shadows with their inventions and gadgets. Moving pictures were flickering across silver screens. Aeroplanes, motor cars, wireless – all were poised on the threshold of the century and would sweep away much of the old order for ever.

It has been said that where and when you are born decides what you are going to do in later life. Did events in the year 1901 influence the lives of Bebe Daniels and Ben Lyon? In Britain and America, inventors like Edison (who said: "We will make electricity so cheap that only the rich will be able to afford candles"), Bell, and Bebe's cousin Lee de Forest were busy with sound machines, the phonograph, kinetoscope, pioneering the telephone, gramophone records and motion pictures. The Italian-born scientist Marconi was developing *his* invention, wireless telegraphy. In 1901 faint signals were heard between Cornwall and Newfoundland.

If a crystal-gazer could have foretold the future of Marconi's wireless telegraphy with worldwide radio transmissions, he could have revolutionized the cult of crystalgazing by linking Bebe and Ben's names with Marconi's gadget. But no crystal-gazer was on hand when Bebe and Ben were born. Certainly no one beyond their immediate families and friends paid more than normal attention to their birth. Yet one day their voices, talking, singing, sparkling with gaiety and warmth, would be carried across the world on wireless wavelengths. Their voices would be recorded on gramophone records and in the 'talkies'; their images on the silver screen would sweep them into the role of international stars. So, it would seem, where and when Bebe and Ben were born did decide what they would do in later life.

To the public a star arrives. How they arrive can only be told in retrospect. The public is never aware of the early struggles at the time these are happening. Bebe and Ben always seemed to be on top, but they were not favoured by birth or right. They got there the difficult way and they knew only too well the razor's edge of staying at the top. What was entailed in 'arriving' can perhaps be summed up by this book inscription to Bebe from Lee de Forest: 'To my dear Cousin, Bebe Daniels. As one de Forest to another! We have both *struggled* to achieve success. With my love. Hollywood Nov. 11, 1930'.

In 1904, Dr Lee de Forest made the first radio transmission overland; in 1906 came his revolutionary discovery of 'putting the grid in the valve'; followed in 1907 by his first radio-telephone transmission. Within the next five years he built the world's first valve amplifier; and from an aircraft in flight in 1916 he demonstrated the first transmission of voice by radio. Some years later he was the first man to put sound on films, heralding the talkies.

Bebe was a strikingly beautiful woman with great dark brown eyes and blue-black hair — legacies of her Spanish ancestry. She was warm, gay, vivacious, she laughed easily. Ben was handsome with some of the same characteristics. They were fun to be with; but they were hard-working and work was a serious thing. They were always busy and kept everyone around them busy. Bebe wrote wittily, humorously, and people often thought she and Ben were like this most of the time in real life. But life was also serious and when it came to business they were business-like.

Bebe and Ben were Americans who became Anglo-Americans, giving to both countries a friendship which the Americans would never forget and the British would always remember. They were never controversial people. But if there was anything enigmatic about them, this was the enigma: that they rose to stardom in America in the silent film era and remained stars throughout the golden years of Hollywood; yet they chose to settle and work in war-torn and post-war Britain.

Ask a younger generation what the names Bebe Daniels and Ben Lyon mean to them. They will recall being allowed to stay up longer than they should, or dashing home in time to listen on radio or watch on television the family programme 'Life With The Lyons', with Bebe, Ben, and their children, Barbara and Richard. They will remember them with the same enthusiasm as those other 'greats' of films – Harold Lloyd, Humphrey Bogart, Gloria Swanson, Maurice Chevalier, Bette Davis, Clark Gable... They were two show-biz troupers whose business was to make people happy and laugh. They succeeded.

In the year 1901, a new century woke up and rubbed its eyes. In seven short decades the world would pass from the 'peaceful Edwardians' into two world wars and then into a technological age which took men on to the moon. In the same life span, from 1901 to 1971, Bebe Daniels, with her husband Ben Lyon, was destined to play more than a normal role in events that made history. She was destined to become not simply a glamorous film star, but a most remarkable woman.

BEBE

1

On the Road

Bebe Daniels was born in Dallas, Texas, on 14 January 1901, into the rumbustious world of the American travelling stock theatre companies. Travelling stock companies came into being nearly forty years earlier after the American Civil War, described later as "one of the bloodiest civil wars in history". America was torn apart. North fought South; brother fought brother. When at last it was over and men saw reason again, united states were born from civil war; but in the immediate aftermath America was exhausted, so theatre companies began taking their plays to the people. In the years that followed more and more companies took to the road; by the turn of the century, when Bebe was born, between three and four hundred companies were spread across the United States. Bebe's father, Danny Daniels, was the actor manager of his own company; her mother, Phyllis Griffin Daniels, the leading lady.

Years later after World War II in Bebe and Ben's London home in Southwick Street, Paddington, when they brought Phyllis back with them from America, Bebe and her mother would tell stories of those travelling days. Their knowledge not only of the theatre but of American legends and history could raise any historian's eyebrows with envy. Evening at dinner, with candles burning in candelabra on the dining-room table, or afterwards over coffee upstairs in the living room lit softly with table lamps – these were favourite times for them to lead us, their friends, back down the years to the 'road' days.

When Phyllis and Danny started out with their travelling company, things had improved from the earlier days when being a road company was like being a pioneer all over again. In those days it was tough and it could be rough – companies undertaking hazardous journeys with scenery, props, costumes, sometimes through warring Indian country. Some of the places where they played are ghost towns now, with skeleton shacks and gaping holes where once there were doors and windows. But when they were 'alive', girls ran giggling from saloons across dusty streets. Cowboys rode into town; the stagecoach came racing in.

As railroads opened up across the States, travelling became a little easier. Listening to Bebe and her mother, you could see a rather prim-looking train belching a banner of smoke from its funnel; you could hear the clatter of wheels over rails and a deep-throated whistle; you could smell the plush of the carriages; you could feel the intense heat of Arizona or the freezing cold of Alaska — a familiar enough picture when film people told *their* stories and in latter years when films of those days became popular in Britain through television. Perhaps films have epitomized those times too romantically; this is no unusual thing. With the passing years reality is easily romanticized; harshness is softened, like looking at things through a camera filter. But the reality of those early days could be harsh and cruel. Like the pioneers who opened up the West, people of the travelling theatre companies died on the way. Some didn't make it.

In one sense, though, the theatre has never changed. The troupers of those early days after the Civil War were no different from the troupers of later eras. They were artistes who took their artistry to the people.

Certainly things had improved when Phyllis and Danny Daniels set out on the road with their company. Theatres had sprung up in many towns and there were good hotels to stay in. Even so, it could still be tough and rough. It was a time of melodrama, vaudeville, burlesque, and there was a vogue for Shakespeare. Phyllis and Danny specialized in Shakespeare, "but," Phyllis would recall, "vaudeville acts got mixed in with Shakespeare — a lot depended on where you were playing. In some towns Shakespeare went down by itself; in other towns you had to put vaudeville acts between scenes to please the audience." Phyllis didn't agree with this at all. In her view "the play was the thing". She was a talented Shakespearean actress and always referred to herself as "an actress of the legitimate theatre". By this she meant she was never in vaudeville or burlesque. So when Danny started putting in saloon and political jokes, even introducing a ragtime band and vaudeville acts between scenes, she felt he

18

was taking too many liberties with Shakespeare.

Phyllis would say: "Danny thought nothing of putting in a husband and wife vaudeville act between scenes, with the husband and wife throwing custard pies at each other when we were presenting *Romeo and Juliet* for instance."

In one town, Danny put in a custard pie-throwing act just before Romeo's death scene. The stage was covered with custard pies. "I said – Danny how could you?"

"Why not?", asked Danny, "the audience loved it – they howled with laughter!"

"But Danny", Phyllis protested, "Romeo *sat* on a custard pie. When he stood up bits of it were stuck to his pants – it was degrading!"

And Phyllis couldn't recall how many times she had picked her way over custard pies littering the stage as she went on in long gowns to play Shakespearean scenes.

But this was what audiences demanded of the travelling companies. Sometimes they played to cowboys or to miners as rough hewn as the mines they were working. What diversions could a company offer these sometimes tough audiences, who applauded raucously, joined in, and shouted their approval or disapproval? Danny improvised, depending where they were playing. He took the theatre just as seriously as Phyllis. He knew she was an idealist whereas he was the realist. He had to be. They had to make money, fill the theatre – and if audiences demanded rough and tumble acts between Shakespearean scenes they had to be given what *they* wanted. It wasn't like that in every town. They played in places where young ladies had formed Shakespearean societies, "and," Phyllis would say, "we had to be very careful how we presented the plays, otherwise we would get letters of complaint. You see it was many years before it all got sorted out. Companies mixed in vaudeville and burlesque acts with melodrama. Someone who danced in a ballet one night might be singing the next night.

"The arrival of a stock travelling company was a great occasion, often starting with a parade through the town – organized by a 'runner' who went ahead of the company to arrange with the local dignitaries the details of the parade. It usually started at the railway station. Everybody turned out to see the parade and join in; sometimes it was almost as big an event as the theatre shows. And people had to do all sorts of things to advertise themselves.

"There was the story of one actor-manager who specialised in melodrama. It was in the days when men wore tall stove-pipe top hats – so tall." Phyllis would hold her hand a good foot and more above her head. "This particular actor-manager had his stove-pipe hats made even taller than anyone elses'. And he had posters painted of himself standing beside a railway engine in such a way that he and his hat were taller than the engine funnel."

So there they were – these travelling companies for ever on the move, dotted all over the States, taking their plays, their melodrama, their vaudeville, their burlesque, to the people. A company sometimes stayed a week in a town, sometimes only one night – in theatrical terms, a one-night stand. They had one or two stars and permanent supporting characters. One famous 'road' star was Maurice Barrymore, father of Lionel, John and Ethel. Because tastes differed from town to town, plays were constantly changed, which meant being in rehearsals for the next play as well as presenting the current one. The same cast played roles as diverse as *Uncle Tom's Cabin*, *The Three Musketeers*, Shakespeare's *Merchant of Venice*. As they moved on, scenery, props, costumes had to be packed up, moved with them, and unpacked again, but to try to keep it all down to manageable proportions scenery was often painted on both sides of 'flats'. There might be a garden scene on one side and the desert on the other side. In the middle of the production with the curtain down for change of scene, instead of sliding another flat on quietly the scenery already on stage was turned round. It was a case of all hands on deck – turn the scenery as quickly as possible. The 'noises off' can only be imagined!

Star attractions often included a politician as part of a company's production. The public would pay to come and hear him speak; or it would be announced on posters that a politician would be in the audience. He was given a box, or a prominent seat and people flocked to see him. Sometimes he was a bigger draw than the play, and the audience watched him with much more interest than the action on the stage. Or Indians would be brought into the audience for a play about Indians. The audience had much more fun watching the Indians' reactions to themselves on the stage, war whoops and all, than watching the play. As well as theatres, there were the Chautauqua — tent shows, so called from the Indian word 'tent'. Companies brought their own tents, like the circus coming to town. The big central tent in which plays took place was often surrounded by smaller tents used as dressing rooms and in which some of the artists lived. When Sarah Bernhardt toured America she had an enormous theatre tent seating several hundred people. And it all had to be transported by train.

In the days of Henry Irving and Ellen Terry it was fairly simple. Irving had his own train and everyone lived on the train. He occupied one coach, Ellen Terry another; the company, scenery, props and costumes occupied all the other coaches.

For a long time the star system flourished. At one period it was the star and very little scenery. A star often rewrote Shakespeare, for instance, so that he got vast speeches and his stock players merely supported him. When Edmund Kean toured America, he did quite a lot of this rewriting. Later, the star system with little or no scenery changed and scenery became very important. How the travelling companies ever moved themselves and masses of scenery from town to town is difficult to imagine, but they did. It took an intrepid company to feature *Hamlet*, carting all round the country the wood to assemble and reassemble the castle of Elsinor.

It was against this background of the travelling theatre that Bebe Daniels was born. Phyllis and Danny were on their way to Waco, Texas. They stopped off at Dallas, Texas, because Phyllis was expecting her first baby. While she waited for the baby's birth she read a book, *Two Little Wooden Shoes*, and she liked the name of the child heroine — Bebe. Besides, Bebe (pronounced *bébé*) meant baby in Spanish. When her baby girl was born, that is what she named her. She was christened Bebe Virginia Daniels.

When Bebe was ten weeks old, her father proudly carried her on the stage. There was no part for a baby in the play, but that did not deter Danny. In the middle of a serious speech, Bebe pulled her father's nose. It brought the house down! Thereafter, whenever a play called for a baby, Bebe was in it. When it didn't, Danny wrote one in.

So for ever on the move from town to town, living on trains and in hotels – packing, unpacking – presenting their plays to the people – this was the kind of early life Bebe knew with her mother and father. But it was by no means the whole story of her background and ancestry.

2

Little Mother

Semper Paratus – Always Prepared

This is the crest of the Griffin family from whom Bebe was descended on her mother's side.

Unlike Bebe, neither Phyllis nor Danny was born into the theatre. Phyllis was born in the American Consulate, Bogota, Colombia, South America, where her father, Colonel George de Forest Griffin, was the American Consul to Colombia. Her mother, the daughter of Colombia's Governor, was descended from a noble Spanish family. She was Eve Guadeloupe de Garcia de Hidda de Hadda Solga Palagas de la Plaza. In later years Bebe, who spoke excellent Spanish, used to run the name off her tongue and she often told her grandmother, 'Little Mother' as she was affectionately called, "Little Mother, they would never get your name in lights!" – meaning theatre lights. Bebe's grandmother was called 'Little Mother' because she was petite, "she was all of four feet eleven" Bebe would say, and because, after her husband died, she became head of the family in true Spanish tradition.

Little Mother's story, as Bebe would tell it, began like a fairy tale. Once upon a time in Bogota, Colombia, a marriage was arranged between Colonel George de Forest Griffin and Eve Guadeloupe de Garcia de Hidda de Hadda Solga Palagas de la Plaza; but almost on the eve of his wedding the Colonel was ordered to go on a mission to the interior of Antiguo and he had to leave immediately. In those days Spanish marriage customs were very strict, so the wedding had to take place without the bridegroom. Little Mother was, in fact, married by proxy but not in any ordinary way. The ceremony took place with all the guests and with Little Mother dressed in her white bridal gown, her dark hair crowned with a beautiful white lace mantilla. She took her vows in church as if her bridegroom were at her side. As she left the church, her family and friends showered her with flowers and the wedding feast followed. At the same time as Little Mother was making her vows in the church in Bogota, George de Forest Griffin made his vows in a church in Antiguo. And so they were married. At last George de Forest Griffin came home and claimed his bride; they set up home in the American Consulate, Bogota, and like the ending of any fairy tale they lived happily ever after. They had eight children — two sons and six daughters, including Phyllis, Bebe's mother. Of the others, Alma and Cleme, Bebe's aunts, and Jasper and Jack, her uncles, became important factors in her life. But far the most important was Little Mother with whom Bebe spent much of her childhood; she came to love her dearly.

Among Phyllis's more vivid memories of her childhood in the Consulate were birthday and Christmas parties. But most exciting, "Each year mother and father celebrated their wedding anniversary with a gathering of family and friends. I can't tell you ... such comings and goings all day ... presents and flowers arriving. And in the evening a dinner party. We children were sent up to bed before the guests arrived, but we were allowed up to see the table when it was finished."

Without Phyllis saying so, but from her description, the gathering had all the hallmarks of wealth and nobility. The Griffin family crest 'Semper Paratus' emblazoned fine hand-made lace-woven table linen and napkins, china, glassware and cutlery. The Colonel presided at one end of the table, Little Mother, petite and elegant, at the other. Candles glowed along the table in silver candelabra. Servants, soft footed and discreet, waited at table. The excellence of food and wine matched elated Spanish conversation. The children were supposed to be in bed, but they didn't stay there. They crept out to watch the comings and goings through the banisters on the landing, until the last guest had gone and they spirited themselves back to their beds.

Such was the background of the Griffin side of Bebe's family.

Phyllis was still a child when her father's term as consul in Bogota expired and he made plans to return to North America. In North America the family would settle in Los Angeles, California. But before they could embark on the sea voyage which would take them finally to Los Angeles they had to cross the Andes. The only way over the mountain ranges was by muleback, and this was how Little Mother, her husband and children made that hazardous journey. As they picked their way along slippery mountain tracks, the children riding their mules straddle legged with no saddles, Little Mother told them, "Don't look down – look upwards to the peaks and heaven. God and St Christopher will take care of us."

In Los Angeles they settled in a town house, a big rambling house of that period with plenty of room for a young family. Here, Colonel George de Forest Griffin, his consular life now terminated, wrote Bancroft histories. He devoted all his time to these writings, later preserved in American history libraries. He died in Los Angeles.

Little Mother was left to bring up the children. She was a typical woman of that period, not businesslike and not expected to be involved in business matters. The Colonel left her a great deal of money, but she was so badly advised that she lost two fortunes. As time went on, far from being deterred by this, Little Mother found means of bringing up her children according to her traditions as a Spanish noblewoman. And such is the Spanish pride that however badly Little Mother was hit by misfortune, nobody ever knew. Phyllis, and in her turn Bebe, inherited this kind of pride. If misfortune hit them, the world would never know.

Phyllis, Alma, Cleme, Jasper and Jack – all the children inherited from their mother and father the kind of qualities which took them to universities and into successful careers. Cleme, in later years, owned a school.

When Phyllis was in her teens, amateur theatricals were the vogue and she, with her brothers and sisters, joined an amateur theatrical society. They became semi-professionals, putting on shows for charity. This kind of entertainment, as well as dances and musical evenings at home, were popular with young people.

At one period when Little Mother was short of money, Phyllis was offered a part in the professional theatre. A producer had seen her in an amateur show and was impressed by her performance. She dashed home full of excitement.

"I've been offered a part in a play," she told Little Mother, "and money!"

At first Little Mother was very much against this. Families might dabble in amateur theatricals, but in the professional theatre, No! In those days the theatre wasn't 'quite nice'. Nobody could say exactly why; the prejudice existed. However, Phyllis won her mother over; the family needed money and here was a chance for her to earn some. So Little Mother, much against her wishes, allowed Phyllis to take the job. Phyllis was a success and Little Mother agreed, reluctantly, that she could go on. Then she met Danny Daniels, her future husband and Bebe's father. They fell in love and were married.

Danny Daniels' real name was Melville Daniel MacMeal. He was the son of an eminent Scottish surgeon and in Victorian tradition of 'like father like son', Mr MacMeal's ambition was for his son to become a surgeon like himself. Many years later, in telling her father's story, Bebe would say: "It was also in those days a tradition in Scotland that the first son of every generation became a physician or surgeon." Melville had studied at the Royal College of Surgeons in Edinburgh and had passed the examinations to become a practising G.P. But he was not content with the prospect of going into practice as a G.P.

This was the era of progress in surgery. Men like Pasteur and Lister were responsible for saving countless lives with the use of antiseptics. Like science, discoveries in medicine and surgical methods were reaching far beyond the boundaries of countries. Students, doctors and surgeons travelled abroad to study new techniques. America was one of the forefront countries. What was happening there fascinated young Melville MacMeal. He persuaded his father to let him go to America and he set sail for New York. It is perhaps not difficult to imagine the bright-eyed young doctor leaning on the deck rail, dreaming of his name becoming as famous as Pasteur or Lister as the steamship rode its way across the Atlantic towards the New World.

But New York was very different from the more staid city of Edinburgh. Theatres were booming and to help out his allowance, Melville took a job in his spare time in a theatre. The acting bug began biting him.

Back in Edinburgh, Mr MacMeal waited patiently to hear from his son, but letters could take weeks to arrive from New York. So he thought little of it — obviously the lad was too busy with his medical studies to write home. Then a letter arrived. Anticipating an enthusiastic and interesting report, Mr MacMeal sat down at the desk in his surgery and opened the letter. He was smiling, but as he read on the smile gradually faded, changing to an expression of utter disbelief. The gist of Melville's letter was: "I have decided to give up medicine for the theatre." *And* he had taken his middle name 'Daniel', added an 's', and would be known in future as Danny Daniels.

If Mr MacMeal had been given to apoplexy he would have choked. Instead, he stood up and paced up and down the surgery floor, his hands clenched behind his back, his chin, adorned with a handsome beard, buried in his chest. Thunder creased his forehead. Now and again he stopped to look down at the open letter on his desk, as if he hoped it would disappear simply by his glaring at it. But it sat there, mocking a father's ambitions for his son. At last Mr MacMeal sat down at his desk, pushed Melville's letter on one side and pulled a sheet of notepaper from a tiered oak writing compendium. He dipped his pen into an inkwell and started writing, stopping occasionally to think out a phrase. Waves of anger flowed from his mind to the pen nib scratching across the paper. It seemed a long time before Mr MacMeal finally signed, "Your father." The gist of *his* letter was: "I forbid you to go into the theatre. Unless you return immediately to your medical profession, I shall disown you. If you defy my wishes, it will be over my dead body — *not* while I live! I repeat — I *forbid* you to continue this iniquitous course."

As Bebe said, "My father turned to the stage and was promptly disowned by *his* father. The disgrace of going on the stage was too much!"

Mr MacMeal addressed the envelope, licked it, smacked it shut and stuck a one penny stamp on it adorned with Queen Victoria's head.

When Melville received his father's not unexpected letter, he had a few pangs of conscience; but by now he was committed. He was soon to be involved in forming his own travelling stock company. America would open up for him on the road. So the dreams of Melville MacMeal, prospective surgeon, of becoming another Pasteur or Lister changed later to his becoming a David Belasco or Oliver Morasco, impresarios of his day, with the glittering prospects of fame not in medicine but in the theatre.

Then he met Phyllis Griffin. After they married and were on the road, the coming of motion pictures presented no threat to them. People said of motion pictures "they won't last", and the theatre went on its way.

3

"I'll Never Stoop That Low!"

Bebe was never one of those children who played a butterfly or a cowslip or a worm wriggling across the stage in school plays, so beloved in the Joyce Grenfell monologues of her imaginary schoolchildren. At the age of four, Bebe was playing the youthful Duke of York in Shakespeare's *Richard III* in her father's stock company. She was billed as 'the youngest Shakespearean actress in the world'. In later years she would say, "I was one of the princes in the Tower. It was my first speaking part. I was smothered after four lines."

The year 1905. The curtain was almost ready to go up in the theatre of Kenton, a town in Ohio, for the opening night of *Richard III*. Backstage there was all the usual last-minute bustle. As actor/manager, Danny Daniels was not only playing Richard III, he was responsible for the production and for seeing that the cast was ready on time. Danny was already dressed, his trained eye checking last-minute details on and off stage. His voice cut through the general bustle.

"Everyone dressed? Where are the beginners?" Danny rapped out the phrases as he rapped them out dozens of times. The phrase "Beginners please!" was echoed in dressing-room corridors by one of the cast in a minor role who acted as call boy.

In the wings, standing back so as not to be in the way, Bebe had been watching the last-minute preparations. All the palpitating magic of backstage activity never failed to fascinate her. The smell of greasepaint was in her nostrils.

Danny spotted her. "Good girl – you're dressed in good time. Know your lines?"

"Yes, daddy." She had rehearsed them over and over again with her mother.

Danny smiled, patting her cheek. "That's my girl. Where's your mother?"

Bebe pointed towards the region of the dressing rooms. "She's coming."

Phyllis hurried towards them and took hold of Bebe's hand. "Darling, I've told you – always wait for me."

Bebe had slipped out of the dressing room she shared with her mother while Phyllis was changing into her costume behind a screen.

"She's okay," said Danny. "Just don't let her get in the way."

"She won't." Phyllis drew Bebe well back into the wings as the curtain went up. As the young Duke of York she was a great success with the cast and audience.

Then disaster. She caught typhoid fever. This episode was one of Bebe's vivid childhood memories.

"I was very ill, with a raging temperature. I can just remember the stage spinning round; the next thing, I was in bed in our hotel bedroom and the doctor was saying to mother, 'she must have her hair cut off.' That's what they did in those days if you had typhoid fever – cut off your hair, believing it helped to give you strength. I was terribly upset.

'Don't let them cut off my hair,' I begged mother.

'All right darling, don't worry — I won't.'

"And mother wouldn't let them cut off my hair. She was wonderful. She gave up her part to her understudy and nursed me through."

In recalling her girlhood and womanhood, Bebe often used the phrases, "Mother was wonderful"; "She was a wonderful mother." As she grew up a deep relationship developed between mother and daughter. Phyllis became her constant companion, adviser and confidant. It was the kind of relationship that was an inborn part of Bebe's character; once formed, whether with her family or friends, it was unshakeable.

A year later, Bebe was now five years old, and the family was playing at the Burbank Theatre, Los Angeles, California. The play, *The Girl I Left Behind*, was a Civil War story. Her role was a little coloured boy, a part very different from the young Duke of York in *Richard III*. She was already learning to switch parts as extreme as a prince to a coloured boy.

Ironically, the title *The Girl I Left Behind* came true in real life and Bebe had her first glimpse of unhappiness in marriage. Her father deserted her mother for another woman he had brought into the company.

Bebe was deeply affected by the separation. In later years when she was a star in the theatre, she would recall, "My father used to hang around stage doors waiting to speak to me." She had a great capacity for forgiving and forgetting, "but I could never bring myself to forgive my father." The reason was not what she herself went through, but what her mother had to suffer. "He had violated her feelings too deeply."

Now she and her mother were alone and life started to be a struggle. They got parts on the stage, Bebe playing a little Indian girl in *The Squaw Man*; but as time went on Phyllis 'rested' more than she worked. By now, Little Mother had closed her town house in Los Angeles and had taken a ranch in the beautiful Verdugo foothills, La Crescenta, a few miles to the north of Glendale, not too far from Los Angeles.

When Little Mother learnt that Danny had deserted Phyllis, she said, "The town house is for you. You will open it up at once." So Phyllis and Bebe went to live in Los Angeles. Although they were able to live in a town house, they had very little money, a fact that Phyllis kept from Little Mother and everyone else. Only Bebe shared this secret with her mother. They eked out their money carefully, allowing themselves a maximum of twenty-five cents to spend on a meal between them. Even so, with Phyllis's natural pride she insisted on using china, table napkins and cutlery emblazoned with the Griffin crest for Bebe, just as it had once been used when she was a little girl in that house.

Bebe would recall: "We used to have wonderful games of make-believe, pretending a snack was a banquet. And to the outside world everything was fine." But things became steadily worse and money became shorter. They would never even admit to themselves that they were poor. Such was the pride of their Spanish ancestry.

Through all this, Bebe's education was not neglected. Phyllis saw to that. With her own background of a first-class education, she was cultured and well read. She became Bebe's teacher. On the subject of learning, not only about facts and figures but about life in its broader sense, she would say to Bebe, "Study – but you can only learn by yourself."

During periods when Phyllis got work in the theatre and Bebe 'rested', she went to live with Little Mother on the ranch at La Crescenta.

"It was beautiful there," she would recall. "Little Mother had about twenty-five acres, a few head of cattle, chickens. At the back of the house there was an avocado tree. You could lean out of an upstairs window and pick the avocados. When they were ripe there were hundreds of them."

At La Crescenta, enjoying the open-air ranch life, these were some of the happiest days of Bebe's childhood. One day, Little Mother said, "I have a surprise for you."

Bebe would laugh good-humouredly as she recounted the way her grandmother spoke English with a decided accent. "She would never admit she had any accent at all, but you could cut it with a knife. She used to end certain words with a clipped 'a'. 'I have-a not got-a da accent,' she would say. So the day she had the surprise for me, it sounded like, 'Come-a with me. I have-a da surprise for-a you.' "

Hand in hand they crossed the ranch land, "and suddenly there was Viva."

"He is for-a you," said Little Mother.

Viva was a pony, in Bebe's eyes the most beautiful pony she had ever seen. His name meant 'life' in Spanish. These were days of the golden West – "riding Viva to school . . . Little Mother teaching me Spanish . . . helping take care of the cattle and feeding chickens . . . the earth carpeted with bluebells and red Californian poppies. The main road to the ranch was still a dusty track with wagon ruts."

Then another part in a play would come along and Bebe went back to Phyllis in Los Angeles. By nature she was a happy child, but because she had spent so much time in the company of adults in the theatre she knew the loneliness of being an only child. She longed for a sister and when she was playing in Ibsen's *The Doll's House*, she paid a little Swedish girlfriend to say she was her sister.

On the other hand, back on the ranch, she could be quite a tomboy, riding Viva with the dexterity of a cowboy, climbing trees, "getting all muddied up. And," she would add, "you know something? I never played with dolls." She was at her happiest among animals. She would take a kitten or baby rabbit to bed with her. "Once I tried to take a live chicken to bed with me." She would laugh. "Ever tried taking a live chicken to bed with you?"

In the company of so many adults in the theatre, some of the cast between shows taught her to play cards. Later, when she went to a convent school in Santa Monica, "one of the nuns caught me teaching the kids how to play poker. I had to stay behind after school and write out fifty times – I must not play poker in the convent."

When she outgrew Viva, Little Mother gave her a horse which she named Flaco. She rode Flaco far into the country or down to the local general store with a list of provisions, at the same time picking up any mail. The store was also the post office. It was always exciting when there was a letter from Phyllis saying she would be home in a few days.

Bebe described Flaco as a real Western horse. "He always knew when there was danger ahead and he would stop dead. I remember one day he stopped and I knew something was wrong. Flaco was right. A few yards ahead along the path there was a rattlesnake, coiled, ready to strike if we had gone on. We didn't. We turned back."

And she would tell a story, handed down, of someone who hid from warring Indians in a hollow tree trunk. "A rattlesnake was in the tree trunk. It wasn't coiled so it didn't strike."

As each year passed, Phyllis 'rested' more than she worked. By the time Bebe was eight, things were pretty desperate, and to make matters worse the Child Labour Law was introduced. America, like Britain, was still suffering from the Industrial Revolution and children were being exploited. There was no question of Bebe being exploited, but one clause in the Child Labour Law stated that no child under age was allowed to be employed in the theatre. So this took Bebe off the stage. Phyllis tried to get round it by making Bebe self-employed – taking shares in a threatical company in which they might be working – but this did not succeed. The authorities quickly forced that arrangement to end.

By now, movies were making great strides. One day a friend said to Phyllis, "Why don't you and Bebe go into pictures? The Labour Law doesn't affect children playing in motion pictures."

Phyllis was shocked. Like Little Mother who had once thought that going into the theatre wasn't 'quite nice', so Phyllis thought the same way about going into movies. Whether she worked or not, she belonged to the legitimate theatre. With only nine dollars in her purse, she replied, "I've done a lot of things in my time, but I'll never stoop that low!"

4

Westerns

However little money they had between them, Bebe and Phyllis were convinced something would come along. It did, unexpectedly. Danny had been doing well and out of the blue he sent Phyllis one hundred dollars. She admitted, "I heaved a big sigh of relief." For the time being the financial situation was saved; but as there was no way round the Child Labour Law, Bebe went back to La Crescenta and to school.

Phyllis got intermittent parts in the theatre, until once again there was no work at all. Reluctantly she agreed to think over her friend's advice to go into movies.

"It will be a terrible come-down," she insisted, "but we've got to eat." So she buried her pride as a leading lady of the legitimate theatre and took Bebe to meet Mr Selig who was making movies in Edendale, not far from Los Angeles.

Years later, recalling that day, Phyllis said, "I didn't realize it, but I was taking Bebe to the first appointment that would one day lead her to stardom in films. If I *had* realized it, I would have run all the way. But we don't know these things, do we?"

Mr Selig signed them up right away.

"I liked them," he said. "Phyllis was a fine actress and Bebe . . . well, she was a natural."

The feeling was reciprocal. Phyllis and Bebe liked Mr Selig.

"He was wonderful, the way he helped us," Bebe would say. "You see, acting in movies was so different from acting in the theatre where you *feel* your audience and each audience reacts differently. Mr Selig taught us how to act to a camera — *but* forget it was there. We had to imagine our unseen audience's reactions — so timing movements and actions was very important."

Their first film for Mr Selig was *The Common Enemy*; their joint earnings £1.00 per day. Bebe played the young daughter of a proud Southerner. "In one scene I was on a horse, but when the rushes were shown they couldn't see me because the horse was too big. Later in the film they changed it to a Shetland pony."

Gradually, all Phyllis's doubts about movies were dispelled. She was honest enough to admit, "I was so wrong." She enjoyed the work. "They're such nice people," she said.

Bebe, still only eight years old, was in a seventh heaven in this new world of the movie makers. Then came Westerns. She was so thrilled with this prospect that she promptly changed her reading habits. Brought up as she had been on a great deal of Shakespeare, she read his plays — acting out the parts as she read them. "I was no good at arithmetic," she would say, "but reading was second nature." Now she forsook William Shakespeare for Zane Grey and other authors who wrote about the West.

Her first Western was with Hoot Gibson and she had the great advantage of being able to ride.

"These were the pioneer days of the Westerns," Bebe would explain, "when cowboys chased across the screen and those same cowboys dressed and made up as Indians chased themselves back again. At the end of a scene, the cowboys jumped off their horses, changed into Indian costumes, feathers and war-paint make-up — took the saddles off their horses and galloped into the next scene, riding bareback." She would laugh. "We made films of how the West was won — silently!"

Bebe was always playing a child stolen by the Indians and rescued by the cowboys. In one Western she played a little girl of the Navaho tribe. "In Navaho language," Bebe would explain, "the pronunciation of 'deer' sounds like Bebe." Indians of the tribe came to visit other Navahos who were in the film. When they heard people calling "Bebe" they thought she was a little girl of their tribe whose name was Running Deer. *Their* little girl had gone away to school and died. They spread the news among themselves that she had come back to them. Bebe tried to explain that she wasn't their Running Deer, but they were convinced she was and she couldn't move without squaws following her everywhere, and at night sitting outside the tent in which she slept.

By now Little Mother had forgotten all her old prejudices against the theatre and films. She and Bebe went to see

Westerns in which Bebe appeared, and others featuring cowboy heroes like Tom Mix and his famous white horse, Bill Hart, Bronco Bill. They took cakes with them, munching in time with the action on the screen. Good men fighting the bad men, the good men winning in the end — great characters for grandmother and granddaughter to munch cakes ecstatically as the action became more exciting, accompanied by a lady thumping out appropriate music on a piano to drown the noise of a whirring projector as well as to heighten the excitement.

By the time Bebe was eleven, Phyllis was doing well. The past year had been successful and she now had a regular salary from a film company called Kalem; but as she travelled quite a lot with the company, Bebe spent even more time at La Crescenta with Little Mother.

Christmas was always spent at the ranch with the entire family — Bebe's aunts, uncles, everyone. Bebe would recall how little Mother would sit in a high-backed chair with a big laundry basket beside her. "We all had to put our presents in her basket first and make sure we filled it to the top, otherwise she would have been very upset. When she had opened her presents, we could have ours. It was a tradition — as head of the family this was her privilege. We did it every year. She enjoyed every moment, so did we."

Then came the year when Phyllis was in regular work. She and Bebe — they always pooled their earnings — invested in a modest bungalow in Santa Monica. The first Christmas in the bungalow they invited Little Mother and all the family to spend it with them.

"We were able to do this because the Kalem company had taken some studios near Santa Monica where companies were making movies," Bebe would recall. "Mother was working in the studios so I could be with her again. I got a few child parts as well. I remember how excited I was that Christmas — Mother and I in our own home and all the family with us."

It was short lived. Phyllis waited until after Christmas before she broke the news to Bebe that the Kalem company had closed down on Christmas Eve. Now, out of work once more, Phyllis was faced with the Christmas bills as well as payments on the bungalow.

"We survived!" Bebe would say. "We never regretted that Christmas or what we spent –there would have been no sense in that, it was such a wonderful day. We soon got work and things began to look better again."

Film-making was expanding rapidly. Film-makers found abundant material in stories of America's turbulent years of history; they recreated their own history in the new medium of celluloid – the War of Independence, the Civil War, and the inevitable Westerns.

In later years Bebe and her mother made more Westerns in Arizona.

Arizona is sudden country. From the southern deserts the central mountains rise and fall away into valleys; then sweep on to the northern plateau region. The sun-drenched desert changes to majestic spruce-covered mountains, to streams and lakes and forests. This is Apache country; it is the country of the Grand Canyon and the Painted Desert, so called because of its colours – pink, purple, red, orange. At sunset the great mountain peaks change suddenly from fiery red to soft purple.

In the endless desert, with its artist-brushed wide blue skies and burning sun, there is a place called Monument City. We see it often enough in Western films, this gaunt city, where nature has carved monuments of stone resembling castles and embattlements. Here the film-makers found their natural location for Westerns, for depicting wagons trekking across the desert to the promised land of California. Here the Indians fought bloody battles with the white settlers and their wagon trains.

When Bebe had any spare time from filming in Westerns she would ride out into the desert and find wisdom in its immense solitude. It was here in the desert that the loneliness she had known sometimes as an only child was washed away and she found something else, the value of solitude. She would ride until she found a water hole, "where you could stop to water your horse and if the water was clear and pure, drink it yourself. The desert," she would say, "is a kind and cruel teacher; the sun can bake you in the day; at night it can be very cold."

She grew up to be a Western 'gal'. She rode a Western saddle. "You always sit tall in a Western saddle," she would explain. In the desert she would slice open a melon with her spur, sit down under a yucca tree and eat the melon before riding on. Yucca trees were named by the Spaniards; their upright branches reminded them of Spanish bayonets.

Those days of the West, the legends and folklore stories never left her. She would say, "A cowboy is no good without his boots; in the desert a man is only as good as his horse; he rides for days on end with a horse for his only friend. In Westerns the bad guys in the saloon are going to get the good guy – the hero – as he rides into town; but *he* gets the bad guys before he rides out of town at the end of the film. And," she would laugh, "a cowboy always kisses the girl with his hat on." In Westerns there was the inevitable chase, warring Indians chasing wagons or a stage coach.

"In real life the Indians would have shot the horses pulling the wagons or stage coach and that would have been that. But they couldn't do that in a film. There would have been no story. You had to build action and crisis. The crisis usually ended happily with the hero getting his girl . . . not always though. Sometimes he rode out of town the same lone figure who rode into town."

Working as she often did in films among Indians she learnt about their beliefs, their artistry, their ceremonies, their hopes and fears in a country where the white man had taken over their lands and hunting grounds and was trying to absorb the Indian into a new civilization on hostile and unfamiliar reservations. They taught her many things, including riding horses bareback Indian style.

"I was fascinated by stories of how the West was 'tamed' ", she would say, "and true stories about the Indians and their culture. As I grew older and learned the real truth of how the Indians were driven from their hunting grounds, their villages, their fishing grounds – buffalo no longer roamed the range, Indians were put into reservations – I was one American who felt ashamed of what we did to them. I think a lot of Americans felt that way, but it's too late now and I guess those early white settlers thought they were right." She would shake her head. "But how wrong can you be!"

Days of the West died hard. The bloody wars between the white man, the Apache, the Sioux, Cheyenne, Comanche, great Indian tribes, savage but proud, were not all that long over. The white man was supreme. Studying the Indian tribes, their culture, their way of life, Bebe told stories that could hold you fascinated for hours. "We see some of it magnified in movies," she would say, "in stories of cowboys and Indians, except the Indians are mostly always the villains. I guess we couldn't admit the cowboys could also be villains."

It all naturally followed that those early years and the Westerns she played in were experiences Bebe never forgot. She could also tell vividly other legendary stories of cowboys and Indians; of riding fast horses across prairies; rounding up cattle for drives; stampedes – "I once saw a stampede – it's terrifying"; the Cavalry arriving in time to save the wagon train or stage coach from Indians on the warpath; all the heroics of Westerns.

The West was rich. Wealth was in the land. Migrants of the gold rush of 1848 who had not found gold turned to farming, to breeding cattle. In time the rich, fertile soil and warm, sunny climate produced a different kind of gold: unending acres of wheat, barley, rustling corn. California was to become one of the richest States in the Union. When the early film-makers came there, they found that the sunshine, giving them long hours of light, was perfect for *them*.

5

Journey of Promise

On the morning of 14 January, 1913, Bebe and her mother dressed carefully, putting on their best clothes. It was Bebe's twelfth birthday. Her mother had received a letter from a film company at Balboa Beach. They were casting a film and the director wanted to see Phyllis and Bebe. The last few dollars they had between them would pay their fares with a little left over. But they weren't thinking of that; they were thinking of the prospects of a job. They got up before dawn, both too excited to have breakfast. "Try to eat something," Phyllis urged Bebe, but Bebe was too anxious to get away in case they should be late. It was a roundabout two-hour journey to the studio at Balboa Beach. Mother and daughter examined each other scrupulously. They looked fine. As they shut the front door behind them, dawn was breaking.

"The beginning of a new day, darling," said Phyllis, "Maybe the beginning of a new life for us."

For Bebe this journey was the best birthday present she could have. They were so sure they would get the job; otherwise why should the director have sent for them? During the journey, Phyllis and Bebe exchanged views on what they would do when they got the job. Phyllis had in mind a special birthday present for Bebe. Bebe, childlike, retaliated with fantastic things she would buy for Phyllis.

Workmen on that early train watched mother and daughter with interest. The little girl, her large brown eyes dancing with excitement, holding her mother's hand and talking excitedly. Her mother, smiling, answering the child. Both dressed in their best as if it were midday, not dawn, with not a hair out of place. They didn't often see anyone quite like these two. "Must be going somewhere special," said one workman to another.

They arrived early at the studio and scrutinized themselves in hand mirrors, making sure once more that everything about their appearance was perfect.

"You look fine, honey," said Phyllis.

"So do you, mother." Bebe sat down beside her mother and they waited patiently as the endless minutes ticked away. At last the director sent for them.

"Come on in," he said. He stood up, leaned across a desk cluttered with papers and shook Phyllis's hand. "Glad to meet you Mrs Daniels."

"We've looked forward to meeting you," said Phyllis with her brightest smile.

The director turned to Bebe. "And you're Bebe Daniels?" Without waiting for her to reply, he fingered some papers on his desk. "I've got all the details you sent me — here," he said to Phyllis.

They all remained standing as the director eyed Phyllis and Bebe, sizing them up like cattle. After a few interminable seconds, he shook his head.

"Sorry," he said, indicating Bebe, "she's too young and . . ." he blinked awkwardly at Phyllis, "I'm afraid you're too short. We want someone taller. Sorry you've come all this way . . . Now if you'll pardon me . . ." He fingered the papers again. "I'll keep these on file — for some other time."

They walked away from the studio trying to pretend it didn't matter. There were other days and other jobs. Later, they heard that the parts in the film had been cast the day before.

Phyllis particularly tried to keep up a brave front. This was, after all, Bebe's birthday. As soon as they got back they would go somewhere nice and have something to eat. But before they got home they were caught in a torrential downpour. It happens like that in California. The rain pours down suddenly, soaking everything and everyone. Phyllis and Bebe arrived home drenched, their best clothes ruined. Still they tried to keep up the pretence that it didn't matter, that their ruined clothes didn't matter. When they had dried and changed, Phyllis said brightly: "Now, let's go and eat!"

They couldn't afford anything more than a modest restaurant where snack meals were served and even these turned out to be more expensive than Phyllis anticipated. "I'm not hungry," she said and ordered only for Bebe. Bebe tried to get her mother to share her snack, but Phyllis refused. As Bebe started reluctantly to eat, the food and imminent tears choked her. Suddenly disappointment overwhelmed her; not for herself but for her mother who had tried so hard to make this day — her birthday — so wonderful for her. And here they were in a cheap restaurant, her mother not eating, pretending to be gay, trying not to think of the cost of their ruined clothes. One day, she would make it up to her; she would take her into good restaurants; she would buy her lovely clothes. Fire and brimstone welled up in her. She hated that director who had wrecked everything. In a few hours the little girl of twelve suddenly became a woman.

As if reading her thoughts, Phyllis turned to her, looked at her searchingly, and smiled. "Never mind, darling," she said,

Bebe

Bebe with Harold Lloyd. Bebe looks cautiously at Harold Lloyd's dog as she introduces her chicken to it.

Bebe in her furnished cell during her ten days in jail. Note the bars in background.

Bebe with Rudolph Valentino in *Monsieur Beaucaire*.

Bebe as Rita in *Rio Rita*.

"There are lots more days – lots more birthdays and," she added seriously, "If you think right, everything will be right."

6

Road to Stardom

"If you think right everything will be right." Bebe quoted her mother's line time and time again throughout her life and to her own children. It was a yardstick of right thinking by which she lived and it was proven to her very early on that if she thought right everything would be right.

The little girl who had so dramatically become a woman in that experience of Balboa Beach was now fourteen. On and off, she'd had ten years of theatre and film training. But where was it leading? She and Phyllis were still short of money, the same pattern of being in and out of work continued, and they went on pretending all was well when it wasn't.

All around them, small film companies like the Kalem company which had folded and thrown Phyllis out of work, were closing down. Backing, which some of the small companies had, was often in the hands of ruthless financiers who wanted quick returns. When the returns didn't come quickly, they foreclosed. Such was the fate of some of the early film-makers. But not all – some survived.

By now and out of work once more, Phyllis decided to take Bebe with her to live in Edendale where more established companies like Selig and Keystone had studios. If they lived on the spot there might be more chance of getting work. It was here in Edendale and through a cowboy friend, Jim Kidd, who was working in movies, that Phyllis heard about a new company, a subsidiary of Pathé, who had moved into studios called Norbig. The company was owned by Hal Roach and Dwight Whitney and they were starting to make one-reel comedies.

41

"Their leading man is Harold Lloyd," Jim told Phyllis, "and they're looking for a girl to play opposite him. How about Bebe?"

There were snags. They were looking for a blonde and Bebe was a brunette. At fourteen, was she old enough?

"I'll make myself *look* older," she said, "and I'll tell them I'll wear a wig."

It happened that Phyllis's young sister Alma was staying with them. Alma was fresh out of college; she wore the latest in clothes which fitted Bebe and could make her look just that much older than her fourteen years. The quicker she got over to the studios the better. So she borrowed a blue silk suit, high-heeled shoes and a hat from Alma and, suitably dressed to look at least sixteen, she arrived at the studios.

In answer to Bebe's knock on the door, a voice on the other side called "Come in."

She took a deep breath, walked confidently in, and there was Hal Roach saying, "Why hullo! What can I do for you?"

"I'm Bebe Daniels," she replied. "I believe you're looking for someone like me to play opposite Harold Lloyd?"

During those years of theatre and film training, she had learned to be a good talker when it came to getting a job.

"Hal Roach and I talked for half an hour and at last he said, 'All right, we'll start with four pictures, but,' he looked doubtful for a moment, 'we were looking for a blonde.' "

"I'll wear a wig!"

Hal Roach shook his head.

"For me you're fine as you are. We'll see what Harold says."

He took her to meet Harold Lloyd and without hesitation *he* said "She's wonderful!" There was no more talk about a blonde, but money had to be talked over. Hal Roach took Bebe back to his office to meet his partner Dwight Whitney and they talked money. Bebe asked for thirty-five dollars a week. Hal countered with twenty-five. The veteran fourteen-year-old asked, "What about clothes?" She would have to wear her own clothes with two or three changes a week. So they settled for thirty dollars a week.

Trying to hide her excitement and be business-like Bebe asked "When do I start?"

"Eight o'clock tomorrow morning."

"What shall I wear?"

"What you're wearing will be fine, but no hat."

Bebe swallowed, stifling a sudden feeling of panic. Suppose Aunt Alma couldn't spare the suit and shoes. She didn't know how long Alma was staying with them. She dashed home as fast as her high heels would allow, with the thought of thirty dollars a week running through her mind. No more money worries, at least for a time! When she got home, Phyllis was out looking for work as usual, and Aunt Alma had also gone out. It seemed an age before she saw her mother return.

"She came into the living room looking so tired and discouraged," Bebe recalled. "She hadn't found any work."

Bebe flung herself into her mother's arms, blurting out her good news and repeating, "Thirty dollars a week — *every* week — thirty dollars! You won't have to work any more!" It was a spontaneous prophecy. She didn't know how many weeks she would work for Hal Roach. She just *felt* that "everything would be right" now.

Aunt Alma returned from shopping and was met with the great news. But what about her clothes?

"Honey," she said, "you can borrow my clothes any time you want, even if I have to stay in bed!"

And so the partnership of Harold Lloyd and Bebe Daniels began with a handshake agreement. No written contract was drawn up until two years later. Even then, as Bebe was still under age, Phyllis had to sign the contract. The partnership lasted four years. Together Harold Lloyd and Bebe made about three hundred one-reel and two-reel comedies at the rate of one new film a week. For a long time these films were made out of doors on location.

"We all went out in cars," Bebe would recall, "with Hal Roach in the leading car not knowing what we were going to shoot, and we worked out ideas on the way. When Hal found a location he liked, we stopped, the camera was set up and he would decide on the scene and action.

"We had no scenarios or scripts; most of it was worked out as we went along, and a great deal depended on what we called sight gags. There was no dialgoue to put over a situation, so we had to react with facial expressions and actions – and a scene was gradually built up to a climax. We didn't learn any lines, though we did a lot of talking. We would say the first thing that came into our heads. But if you watch silent movies carefully, you'll see how much depends on the action and sight gags.''

In all the three hundred comedies they made, Harold Lloyd contributed many ideas. As time went on and Bebe learnt more and more about comedy situations, she gradually put in ideas.

A situation was built up from a simple incident.

For instance: Bebe is innocently watering a garden. She sees her sweetheart Harold approaching and turns to wave at him. As she turns back, still holding the hose, a delivery man has come into the garden. Bebe soaks him. Harold comes on the scene. Bebe, not knowing what to do with the hose, turns to Harold and soaks him. The delivery man goes to the tap but instead of turning off the water he turns it on more, and the hose in Bebe's hand behaves like a snake with water gushing from it. Her father comes out of the house. *He* gets soaked. The hose is still glued to Bebe's hand. She is obviously shouting for somebody to turn off the tap. In the end she soaks everyone and everything in sight before the tap is turned off.

There was the inevitable chase; up and down staircases; in and out of swinging doors with the villian chasing Harold, and Bebe trying to help him but often hindering him and the villain almost catching him. The villain was usually a huge man with a vicious moustache and bristling eyebrows.

These were the days of Buster Keaton, Laurel and Hardy, Chaplin – and the birth of film comedy. If some of it was slapstick, with unlimited whitewash being thrown over people, or paintpots landing on someone's head, or a hole in the ground into which an unsuspecting passer-by disappeared, or a banquet ending in a custard pie duel; all this kept people rocking with laughter in their cinema seats.

And always there were Westerns. Bebe and Harold Lloyd made Western comedies with Bebe playing the Western gal, quick on the draw, rolling her own cigarettes, and Harold playing the diffident hero taking on all the bad men in town – getting into unbelievable scrapes before he rode the bad men out of town and the slow fade of claiming his gal.

They all did their own stunts. Bebe would recall, "If you didn't do your own stunts you didn't get the job." So she did daring scenes on horses, in cars, boats and, later, aquaplaning. She would fall off things and over things. But she drew the line at one thing. "I would take all the falls they wanted me to – but I'd never stand still and let them toss eggs and pies at me."

Doing stunts often landed her in hospital – reported as recovering from a severely strained back or strained ankles.

These were the days of girls in swimsuits with bloomers worn below the knees and adorned with garters and rosettes. The girls dabbled in and out of the sea, splashing each other. Little Mother sewed rosettes and ribbons on Bebe's swimsuits ready for filming. So they turned out film after film. They hired evening gowns; they did their own hair and make-up. Bebe and her friends bought their make-up from a little shop near the studios – the man who prepared this for them was Max Factor.

Wonderful days! Not only working but having fun. "On days when we weren't filming," Bebe would recall, "Hal Roach used to hire buses and take us to Venice (California) or Ocean Park. We took joy-rides on everything at the fairground, rode the roller coasters, played all the games, and we finished off the evenings with hot dogs and popcorn!" Harold Lloyd always sat next to Bebe in the bus or on the roller coasters.

On other days, Bebe and her girl-friends Mary Mosquini and Estelle Harrison went to the movies. The girls were movie crazy, sometimes taking sandwiches with them to the cinema so they could see a film twice over and not get hungry.

So one year passed into the next. And it followed that a boy and girl romance developed between Bebe and Harold Lloyd. He was her first 'date'. By nature he was shy and it took him a long time to pluck up enough courage to ask Phyllis if he could take Bebe out. Phyllis was strict with Bebe as she was still under age. She would not allow her to go out unescorted with a boyfriend. Bebe wasn't bothered. She was enjoying her film work and was happy at home. But Phyllis did agree that Harold could take her to movies and to dances, provided he brought her home "real early".

Bebe and Harold were happy together and at one period very much in love. He asked her to marry him. She was now about eighteen, but in no hurry to marry. Harold agreed to wait. He bought a diamond, had it made into a tie-pin, and if and when Bebe said 'yes' he would have it remade into an engagement ring. The diamond remained a tie-pin.

These were not the money-spinner days, but at least Bebe and her mother were secure. One day, Bebe said to Harold, "The time will come when an actress will make a hundred and fifty dollars a week."

"Oh no," said Harold, "maybe an actress like Mary Pickford. But nobody like you or me."

In time both would become rich as well as famous. Within ten years Harold Lloyd would make over a million dollars a year. But that was in the future. For the moment both were content.

Bebe and Harold became expert dancers and they entered dancing contests at the Old Sunset Inn, Santa Monica. One night Cecil B. de Mille came to a contest. Bebe was wearing a white satin gown. From his table Cecil B. de Mille watched her, this vivacious looking girl dancing with Harold Lloyd. He was always on the look-out for talent and in Bebe he recognized star quality. She and Harold had danced several times when a man came over and said to her, 'Mr de Mille would like to meet you."

Bebe was thrilled. Cecil B. de Mille was already a big name in the film industry, known to everyone as 'C.B.' She and Harold joined him at his table.

"How would you like to come and work for me?", he asked her. Harold looked from one to the other, wondering what she would say. So much was at stake in their set-up with Hal Roach. Bebe realized that Cecil B. de Mille was offering her a great chance; but, as Harold said many years later, "One of her virtues was loyalty."

She thanked Mr de Mille. "I'm afraid I can't accept," she said, "I am under contract to Hal Roach – and," she added, "I'm very happy." Mr de Mille nodded, respecting her loyalty. As they left his table, he said to her, "If and when you are not under contract to Hal Roach, give me a ring at the studio."

At last her contract came up for renewal. Bebe was torn between continuing in comedy or following an urge to become a dramatic actress. Harold Lloyd did everything to dissuade her. "Studios don't take comediennes into drama," he said, but she kept saying, "I know I can be a dramatic actress if someone will give me the chance." She was no newcomer to this kind of thinking. She was the voice of her own youth asking to be given a chance.

Perhaps it is not difficult to imagine the perplexity of Harold Lloyd and Hal Roach. Where was their Bebe going? Did *she* know? With the optimism of the young –she was not yet twenty – she would not be convinced that such an attempted change could be very risky. She told Hal Roach and Harold Lloyd that she had got a job as a dramatic actress, although as yet she had no job. It wasn't that she wanted to leave them, but she had to make the break some time.

She wrote to Cecil B. de Mille, "Are you still interested in me?"

Back came the reply, "Of course. Come over to the studios."

Now came the age-old problem. How should she dress? As a budding dramatic actress? She decided to look sophisticated. This time, instead of trying to look older as she had done when she borrowed Aunt Alma's clothes, she borrowed a suit from her mother, a squirrel cape and a hat with white flowing aigrettes, and off she went to see Cecil B. de Mille.

From the start he made her feel at ease. He sat behind a massive desk and outlined his plans of the kind of films he would be making and how he could see her fitting into them. He explained that he was planning bigger things with Jesse Lasky of the Famous Players-Lasky studios. She listened attentively, hoping in the way she sat and reacted that none of the nervousness she felt came across to the great man. "So," he concluded, "I'm going to offer you a four-year contract." This was more than she could ever have hoped for. She said goodbye to him on a high note of excitement she could no longer suppress. Just as she was leaving his office, he stopped her. "Let me give you a piece of advice."

Bebe turned in the doorway. "Yes, Mr de Mille?"

He was smiling. "Next time you come to see me, don't wear your mother's clothes."

The contract was drawn up at half the salary Bebe was earning with Hal Roach. But it was still a good salary running into three figures a year, and what mattered more than money now was the chance to fulfil her ambition to be in drama. Phyllis signed the contract as Bebe was still legally under age.

After the years of playing opposite Harold Lloyd in the Hal Roach productions, saying goodbye was a sad affair. And although Harold knew that Bebe would never marry him now, they always remained firm friends. Her parting gift from the studios – a string of real pearls, the first piece of jewellery she ever possessed.

And now to work at the Paramount studios under the direction of Cecil B. de Mille. Here it was very different from the small, friendly group which she knew so intimately at the Hal Roach studios. At Paramount everything was done on a much bigger scale, from the size of the studios to the lavishness of productions, with dozens of people milling around. For the first time Bebe had a hairdresser, someone to supervise make-up, and a costume designer. At first she felt lost and lonely, handed on from one to another. Then came the first day's shooting with Cecil B. de Mille. She was cast as a Babylonian's king's favourite in *Male and Female*, playing with Gloria Swanson, and Thomas Meighan as the king. Dressed in yards of chiffon and a heavy silver headdress, "I felt sick with nerves," she hoped any nervousness she showed would be accepted because she had to play near a den of lions, very real and wild. *Male and Female* was a success and Cecil B. de Mille next cast her in *Why Change Your Wife?* again with Gloria Swanson. She and Gloria were the two wives and Thomas Meighan was the husband. At that time Gloria Swanson was Paramount's leading star and Thomas Meighan was equally famous. The result, although they were kind to Bebe, was that she was overwhelmed by them and, unlike the outgiving person of comedy pictures, she became shy and self-conscious, tending to sit alone in her dressing room until she was needed for a scene.

"I often cried and wished I had never left Hal Roach, or at least had listened to him and Harold when they said, 'You won't be happy at Lasky's.' Then I snapped out of it. This was ridiculous. I had wanted to go into drama. And here I was, wallowing in self-pity." So, with a brave new face and enjoying her work again, her next role was in *Everywoman*. This was followed by two pictures playing opposite Wallace Reid, *The Dancing Fool* and *Sick Abed*, still under Cecil B. de Mille's direction. After the last day's shooting, Jesse Lasky sent for her. All the old uncertainties she had felt when she first joined de Mille welled up again. "Why should Jesse Lasky send for me? Was he going to fire me?" She arrived at his office, trying to appear relaxed and casual.

"Sit down," said Jesse Lasky. She sat and waited.

"Mr de Mille and I have been talking things over . . ."

Bebe smiled stiffly. *Here it comes*, she thought.

". . . about your future with us."

"Yes?" Bebe nodded, still smiling, but she was thinking, *Well go on, get it over.*

"We have decided to . . ." Bebe sat rigid. ". . . star you."

"*Star* me! Oh Mr. Lasky, I thought . . ."

"What did you think?" The voice belonged to Cecil B. de Mille. He had been standing behind a screen; now he stepped out, smiling broadly. "How's that for a surprise?"

"Wonderful! . . . Just wonderful! Thank you."

"Now let's see," said de Mille. "You've been with us six months. We're going to tear up the four-year contract and draw up a new five-year contract with Realart which you may or may not know is a subsidiary of the Famous Players-Lasky. How does that sound?"

"Sounds great! I can't believe it. Me – starring *me* as a dramatic actress!"

De Mille shook his head. "No – not as a dramatic actress."

"No?"

"No – as a comedienne."

In later years Bebe said, "Every time I wanted to go into drama they put me back into comedy."

For the next two years she starred as a comedienne in films with titles like *Two Weeks With Pay, Old Wild Week, Nancy From Nowhere, Ducks and Drakes.*

Bebe and Ben

After *Ducks and Drakes* was released in 1921, this write-up appeared in a movie magazine:

Bebe Daniels is 5'4" — that is tall enough and we imagine she'll stay that way, though she's quite young. But what we mean is that if she continues to improve as she has of late she is going to be *some* star. 'Ducks and Drakes' is a picture to make anyone take notice. Granted she's pretty. Everyone knows that. But she can act too. If the vamp days weren't all shot, Miss Daniels would have the fans forgetting there ever was a vamp before. A Hollywood informant tells us she's one of the most popular players on the big lots. Everyone loves her, even the whole Ninth Infantry, which has just made her an honorary colonel! Bebe is another product of the comedies.

And somewhere, not recorded, this write-up appeared:

'Ducks and Drakes'
Blue Mouse Theatre, 5th Avenue,
Just South of Pike.
Realart Pictures Film

Taming A Flirt

Her fiancé had just about decided it
couldn't be done.

Here's a mile-a-minute modern comedy drama that gives
Miss Daniels one of those "good little bad girl" roles
which is peculiarly suited to her dashing personality.

Nancy From Nowhere had this caption to three pictures from the film:

Montreal   Avril 1922   Le Film
Bébé Daniels dans TROIS SCENES de Nancy From Nowhere,
production Paramount.

Two years later, Paramout absorbed Realart, "and I was back once again as a dramatic actress."

During the two years with Realart a new interest was introduced into film-making. Stars travelled, making personal appearances with their films. Bebe travelled to places like Houston, San Antonio, El Paso and Dallas, Texas, where she was born. So much had happened in the twenty years since she had been carried on the stage by her father when she was only ten weeks old.

Now she was back with Paramount a more seasoned actress, making films again with Cecil B. de Mille like *The*

Love Affairs of Anatole, followed by *Nice People*, co-starring with Wallace Reid and Conrad Nagel; and once again, the wheel coming full circule, she made Westerns. One of these *North of the Rio Grande* was made in Arizona with Jack Holt. All of them names which have come down in film history annals.

So film followed film with scarcely a break until one day, unpredictably, the shooting of a picture by Paramount in Hollywood was held up while its young star, Bebe Daniels, spent ten days in jail.

7

My Ten Days in Jail

It happened in Orange County, California, in 1921. Jack Dempsey, then heavyweight boxing champion of the world, was dating Bebe. She was high spirited and she loved fast cars. Bebe tells the story as she wrote it.

"One of the things I enjoyed most, when I wasn't making films, was speeding. I had a fast car which, in the twenties, did over seventy miles an hour — quite a speed in those days; and I was constantly being caught by speed cops for driving too fast. Not that I ever had an accident or hurt anyone. But all I had to do when I got a ticket for speeding was to call up my Uncle Jack who was an important newspaper man and 'in' very well with the Los Angeles police department. Uncle Jack would say, 'What's the number of your ticket baby?' — and he would take care of it with the police and pay my fine. I remember once calling him up and when he asked, 'How many tickets this week baby?', I said, 'Three.' Uncle Jack replied, 'Only three! Baby, you're slipping.'

"So I continued speeding, knowing that my Uncle Jack could always take care of it, until one day I took a trip to San Diego with my mother and Jack Dempsey. The route from my home just outside Hollywood, Los Angeles, was along the highway through Orange County, so named originally because of its thousands of acres of beautiful orange groves. In parts of California the orange groves were vast and pungent. Even flying over them at five thousand feet in an open cockpit plane of those days, you could smell their fragrant scent.

"But to come back to earth and the open road from Los Angeles to Orange County. I was driving and the speedometer ticked up to seventy-two miles an hour, a crazy speed in the twenties; but no other car was in sight. Then suddenly I heard a siren, and two motor-cycle policemen roared up alongside and flagged me down. The usual ticket followed.

"One policeman said, 'You know we put people in jail for going this fast.' I replied, 'Oh, don't be silly.'

'As soon as we got to the next town, Santa Ana, in Orange County, I telephoned Uncle Jack.

" 'What's the trouble now baby?', he asked

" 'Just another ticket,' I replied.

" 'Where are you?'

" 'Orange County.'

" 'Baby, you're in the wrong County,' he said.

"I asked him what he meant. He told me that Judge Cox, who was the Judge of Orange County, put everyone in jail who drove over fifty miles an hour. He had even put an Admiral of the American Navy in jail. Quite undaunted I said, "Well you can fix it, can't you Uncle Jack?' But this time Uncle Jack couldn't fix it.

"In America, the different states are divided into counties. Each county has its own court and rules and runs its local affairs rather like boroughs in England. The counties are divided by a boundary line, sometimes marked only by a signpost. And on this day as I sped along the highway at over seventy miles an hour and crossed the boundary line into Orange County, I knew nothing about Judge Cox or his fifty miles an hour speed limit – and I drove straight through a police trap.

"Later I learnt a great deal about the Judge. He was known as the Nemesis to speeding motorists, and his word was law in Orange County; but at this moment I was much more concerned with a summons to appear before him in the County Court House in Santa Ana.

"My lawyer insisted that I should be tried by a jury. As I was under age, he was convinced I would be let off. The trial was in the true Perry Mason tradition. I sat with my lawyer in the well of the Court; the prosecuting attorney sat on the other side of the middle aisle; and Judge Cox faced us from the bench. Behind us were rows of public and Press. The court was packed, standing room only, with the usual mixture of well-wishers and curiosity seekers.

"The prosecuting attorney presented his case and called the two motor-cycle policemen to the stand. They illustrated their speed trap with diagrams on a blackboard, and finally presented their stop watches to the jury for inspection. There was no doubt that I was doing over seventy miles an hour.

"As Judge Cox listened to the evidence, he was looking at me with a smile, and I smiled back at him. I continued smiling at him when I was called to the witness stand, thinking he would let me off with a warning and a fine. At that time I was working for Paramount film studios and they had already sent a thousand dollars to the Court to pay any fine. So I was not in the least bit worried; but Judge Cox's smile proved to be very deceptive.

"From the witness stand, I returned to my seat beside my lawyer and we waited for the jury's verdict, which of course was 'guilty of exceeding the speed limit'. Judge Cox rapped his gavel sharply on the bench. My lawyer and I stood up. The Judge looked across at me, smiled again, and to my horror said, 'You are sentenced to ten days in the Orange County Jail.'

A wave of protesting whispering broke out in the Court and flashlights went off from photographers' cameras. They were photographing the Judge and me, and the trial received countrywide publicity. Afterwards, I learnt that the Judge revelled in this sort of thing. He never 'turned his back to a camera', and he thoroughly enjoyed seeing his name in print.

"He did, however, give me time to finish the film I was making for Paramount in Hollywood. This took about three weeks; then I went back to Santa Ana to serve my ten days in jail. My mother came with me. She was wonderful. She said, 'If you're going to jail honey, so am I.' As I had been sentenced for a misdemeanour, not a crime, my mother was allowed to stay in my cell with me, and I was also allowed to wear my own clothes.

"As the newspapers were full of the trial and sentence, furniture companies started bidding to furnish my cell before I arrived at the Santa Ana jail. When I heard about this, naturally I chose the best furnishing store in town. At the same time, restaurants were also bidding to serve my meals gratis. So I chose the best restaurant.

"When my mother and I finally arrived at the jail my cell was furnished with wall to wall carpet, chintz curtains, and an attractive bedroom suite with twin beds and covers to match the curtains. There were even bedside tables and lamps.

"Neither Judge Cox nor the jailer could stop all this. A person sentenced for a misdemeanour was allowed privileges, although I hardly think the Judge or the jailer expected anyone to have quite these privileges. But in fact, I think Judge Cox secretly loved every bit of it. He was even waiting for me on the steps of the jail when I arrived to welcome me with a bouquet of flowers, and photographers were there to record the event. The Judge saw me to my cell rather like an hotel manager, saying as he did so, 'I hope you will be very comfortable.' As I walked into my cell, I was greeted with banks of flowers, sent by my movie star friends, and the cell looked like a florist's shop.

"But I shall never forget the ominous sound of locks being turned and iron gates clanking behind me, and the sound of my cell door being locked on my mother and myself. Despite the lavish furnishings and the flowers and the excellent food that would be served by the best restaurant in town, I was really very miserable. It was a terrible feeling to be locked in one room, even though it was beautifully decorated and my mother was with me. However, I was so furious with Judge Cox that I would not allow myself to cry.

"These were the 'roaring twenties' and the days of prohibition and bootlegging in America. I learnt that Orange County was quite a hotbed for bootlegging. It has a long coastline and bootleggers used deserted coves to try to smuggle in liquor after dark from Mexico.

"A few hours after we arrived at Santa Ana jail, the jailer

brought a woman to my cell. 'This is Sadie,' he said. 'She's asked to clean your room every day for you.' Sadie was quite a girl. 'What are you in for?' I asked her. She smiled sheepishly and replied, 'Bootlegging.'

"I did not have to keep any regulations about times to get up or to have meals. Mornings began when I woke up and this could be any time between six and seven o'clock. I was used to waking up early because in films we had to be dressed and made up and on the set by nine o'clock, so my usual time for getting up was around six o'clock.

"The jailer and his wife were sweet people. The jailer's wife allowed my mother and me to use her private bathroom. After we had taken our baths and dressed and were back in our cell, breakfast was served. This consisted of coffee, grapefruit, scrambled eggs, bacon, hot rolls — anything we wanted — brought in from the restaurant by an impeccable waiter dressed in a morning suit. He stayed in the cell and served all our meals in the best luxury hotel manner.

"After breakfast, mother and I read the morning papers, magazines or books. I was an avid reader, and I read plenty.

"There was no exercise period and I used the cell window bars to pull myself up and down to keep fit. One of the things one has to fight in a locked cell is the inclination to pace up and down like an animal trapped in a cage. So some form of exercise was vital.

"I also had to fight constantly looking at the time. At first I did this quite a lot and time dragged interminably. They were long mornings, until at last the jailer turned the lock, opened the door, and the waiter wheeled in a trolley with our lunch — a choice of salad, meat and vegetables, sweet, cheese and coffee. For lunch the waiter changed his morning suit for a white jacket and black bow tie.

"The afternoons passed more quickly. My movie star friends were determined to keep me bright and cheerful. Not only did they send in fruit and chocolates and fresh flowers daily, but I had a flood of visitors every afternoon. Many of my friends came from Hollywood to see me — quite a trip. I even kept a guest book. The jailer always brought my visitors' cards before he showed them in. One day he said with a long-suffering sigh, 'This is more like a summer hotel than a jail.' On one occasion the jailer presented me with a calling card of someone I didn't want to see. I said, 'Tell him I'm out.' The jailer shook his head, 'Miss Daniels, I can hardly do that.'

"Then one day I heard music coming from below my cell window. I climbed on a chair, held on to the bars and looked out. Down in the courtyard was Abe Lyman and his Orchestra. They had come from the Coconut Grove in Los Angeles just to serenade me, and they were playing 'Rose Room Tango', my favourite tango number. In those days I always danced the tango at the Coconut Grove with Rudolf Valentino. Abe knew this. The orchestra stayed all afternoon and got through quite a repertoire of my favourite numbers.

"But each afternoon when the last visitor had gone, I had a pretty bad let-down feeling. It was like waving goodbye to friends going off on a trip and you are left standing on a platform as the train steams away. You don't quite know what to do with yourself.

"At last dinner-time came and, to ring the changes, the waiter wore full evening dress – tails, white tie, the lot. Dinner was the highlight meal. The restaurant really went to town, and they sent in a wonderfully varied menu, anything from fillet steak, fried chicken, mushrooms, crayfish, lobster, fillet sole, and sometimes even caviar!

"It must have been the strangest jail sentence ever, and I began to notice that the poor jailer was getting more confused and tired looking every day; but he was a good sport and he allowed mother and me to go out each evening after dark for a walk. We went to a playground in a park across the road. And there I went on the swings and a seasaw. But I had to be back in my cell by ten o'clock with the lights out, and each night I had the recurring feeling of how awful it was to be locked in a cell.

"At last the sentence was coming to an end, and to my relief I was given one day off for good behaviour. So I only had to serve nine days, the longest nine days I have ever spent in my life. The jailer confided to me that they were the busiest days he had ever spent and he was exhausted.

"Living up to his reputation for seeking publicity, Judge Cox came to my cell and presented me with another bouquet, this time roses, to set me free and wish me every happiness. He insisted on photographs being taken with me as he presented the bouquet. This goodbye scene with the Judge was widely reported in the newspapers, which pleased him immensely. That was the last time I ever saw him and, needless to say, the last time I ever broke a speed limit, at least in real life. But, as no experience is ever lost, I made a film afterwards called *The Speed Girl* based on the story of my ten days in jail. I played the lead and went to jail again, but thank goodness this time it was only make-believe."

The Speed Girl, with a picture drawing of Bebe in a sports car going at the speed of a rocket and the car looking like one, had its World Premiere at the Kinema, Los Angeles. The write-up said, "Here is a six cylinder hundred and twenty fun powered record-breaking comedy with Bebe at the wheel. The brakes are off. Slip her into high. Now step on it!"

Bebe stopped speeding in fast cars for another reason. "One night," she said, "I'd had a dream – I was passing a white house and some people I had known who had died came out of the house and beckoned me in. I don't remember the end of the dream. A few days later, I was speeding as usual and I was wearing one of those floating chiffon scarves tied round my neck. It was an open car with the wind blowing the scarf all over the place, and suddenly it blew across my eyes as I was approaching a curve. I pulled it away just in time to avoid crashing as I sped round the curve, braking. I stopped the car and right there, a few yards off the road, was a white house, exactly like the one I had seen in the dream. It was a warning, it really was, so what with that and going to jail, I stopped reckless driving."

8

Cecil B. de Mille

Paramount waited for Bebe to leave jail and she went on to make more films with them. The film industry was getting better each year in quality and stories. Cecil B. de Mille, who became known as "Mister Hollywood himself", came to the industry as a founder film-maker in 1913 from the theatre. It was now the 1920s and Cecil B. de Mille was leading the way with Biblical epics like *The Ten Commandments* and *King of Kings*. Without doubt he was a great influence on Bebe's career, giving her starring roles and that elusive quality – glamour – which became so much a part of the Hollywood scene.

In the 1920s New York was still a centre of the film industry, and stars went there from Hollywood to make films. Paramount sent Bebe there to star in *Glimpses of the Moon*.

Asked by a newspaper man, "What do stars do when they cry?", when in *Glimpses of the Moon* she had to go through a tearful scene, she replied, "I think of the scene I'm playing and make up poetry of my own – perhaps I'm so bad that I cry. Music helps me too, but I must have something with a sad motif and I prefer just a violin."

Harold Lloyd happened to be in New York at the same time and, as it was Bebe's first time in the city, they 'did' the sights like any other tourists. "We went to Grant's tomb, Wall Street, and of course Broadway."

At that time, Fred Astaire and his sister Adele were also filming in New York. Fred Astaire remembers it well. "It was summer, hot. When Adele and I had finished filming for the day, we used to pick up Bebe and we'd all drive through Central Park in an open horse-drawn cab. It was all a bit like those Central Park settings of romantic movies, and on the way we filled an ice bucket with bottles of soda pop. I can see us now – cooling off in the heat, drinking our ice cold soda pop – singing, laughing . . They were great days."

But all this was short lived. Bebe was taken ill with

appendicitis. In those days, appendicitis could have complications. "If anyone could have complications, I could!" she said. She was on the danger list for several days. At last she was well enough to go to Arizona where, still recuperating, she made *The Heritage of the Desert*.

As soon as she was fit again, back to New York to make *Monsieur Beaucaire* with Rudolph Valentino. She played a French princess, and to quote her, "Although it was a silent film we had to learn the lines in *French* to give correct lip movements. I can't tell you what some of the accents were like — mine too!

"People asked me about Rudolph Valentino's temperament — he was supposed to be temperamental. But I never saw it. He was a charming man, intelligent, with a marvellous sense of humour, wonderful to work with. I remember he went to Italy for a holiday — he was born in Italy — and I said to him when he got back, 'I guess everyone recognized you on the streets?'

" No,' he said, 'I was just another wop!'

"I tell you, I wouldn't have missed *Monsieur Beaucaire* and acting with Rudy for anything in the world."

It was the vogue for stars to teach the latest dancing steps in illustrated journals. Bebe and Wallace Reid wrote, with pictures, a jazz dance series explaining the steps. Rudolph Valentino's name became associated with the tango. He and Gloria Swanson did a similar series explaining the tango. And of another dance, the shimmy, Rudolph Valentino wrote, "If you must do the shimmy, do not shake the shoulders. Shake only the hips — but only gracefully, lightly. Otherwise the shimmy is vulgar and suggestive."

When he died, Bebe bought much of his collection of guns, costume books, seventeenth-century Italian plaques and swords when these were auctioned. "I did this," she said, "because he loved them so much."

Bebe already had a collection of about one hundred and fifty swords which she kept in a special room in her Santa Monica home. Among these was a sword brought to America by Columbus. Another was owned by a Crusader. Yet another dated back to the eighteenth century. To these she added the Rudolph Valentino collection. The reason for her interest in swords was that she was an expert fencer and a member of the Amateur Fencing League of America. One year the League wanted to enter her for the Olympics. Reluctantly she had to turn this down because she was busy filming.

Still only in her early twenties, she was written up and interviewed in newspapers and journals in many parts of the world. Her films were shown in far-away places like Montevideo, Havana, France, Britain, Spain, Tokyo, with cinema billings and write-ups in those languages. "Try pronouncing Bebe Daniels in Japanese," she would say laughingly.

Browsing through hundreds of press cuttings in different languages, I rather liked this write-up in the *Telegram*, Milwaukee, Wisconsin, April 1923:

> The names of a cluster of far famed film stars will flicker forth from the electric lights in the city this week – Norma Talmadge in 'The Voice from the Minaret' to be shown at the Strand; Lionel Barrymore in 'The Face in the Fog' at the Garden Theatre; Bebe Daniels and Lewis Stone should be quite a fascinating combination in 'The World's Applause' at the Alhambra.

Well – that was the 1920s that was!

And if your favourite magazine thinks up a Personality Quiz, they were doing *that* in the 1920s as well. Bebe answered this one in April 1922:

What is your favourite virtue?	Strength of character
Your favourite quality in women?	Good morals
Your favourite quality in men?	Refinement and manliness
Your favourite occupation (next to the Screen)?	The Stage
Your idea of happiness?	To be able to adapt myself to circumstances
Your idea of unhappiness?	Being dissatisfied
Your favourite colour?	Orchid
Where do you prefer to live?	Any place with my family and friends
Who is your favourite prose author?	Vicente Blasco Ibañez
Who is your favourite poet?	Oscar Wilde
Your favourite hero in real life?	General Pershing
Your favourite heroine in history	Joan d'Arc
Your particular aversion?	Spiders and motor cops

Cecil B. De Mille

What character in history do you most dislike?	Catharine de Medici
Your favourite motto?	Live and let live
Your favourite role?	Satynne Synne in 'The Affairs of Anatol' and Teddy in 'Ducks and Drakes'

(signed) BEBE DANIELS

And this touch of patriotism —
In October 1923 the Governor of Texas asked Bebe to set cotton styles.

> Referring to her as the "most becomingly dressed actress on the screen", Pat M. Neff, Governor of Texas, has written a personal letter to Bebe Daniels, Realart star, asking her to aid in popularising cotton fabrics for women's wear, as a measure to aid the growers who lost so heavily on last year's cotton crop.
>
> Governor Neff refers to Miss Daniels' birth in the Lone Star State (Texas) and asks her help to promote a movement 'Clothes of American Cotton'. Miss Daniels promised her hearty support.
>
> In fact it was well known in the Los Angeles cinema colony that Bebe Daniels, famous for the gorgeous gowns she wears on the screen, in every day life goes to and from the studio in ginghams, organdy or voile dresses.

Of the time she spent in New York, Bebe wrote: "I realize what a wonderful and exciting and warm-hearted place it is. It was there I first met Marion Davies, Louella Parsons and the fabulous William Randolph Hearst."

Then followed a period when she was away from Hollywood for three years, making films in Nassau, Bermuda, Florida. Altogether she made twenty-five pictures for Paramount. In doing her own stunts, she broke bones, tore muscles, was bitten by wild animals. In *Senorita* she nearly lost an eye in a fencing duel with Raoul Paule. Paule was coached — he knew very little about fencing — but he forgot the right moves on the 'take'.

She became experienced in all aspects of film-making. She headed her own unit in Paramount for five years. She was just twenty-four when Paramount gave her this unit with complete supervision of stories, cast and budget. Of the twenty-five pictures she made and wrote with her co-writers, Paramount only bought one. During her last years with them, she was the only woman among a group of twenty top directors and writers on the Paramount 'inner cabinet'.

And a final word about New York. In New York in 1924 Bebe met Ben for the first time. She was introduced to him by Eddie Sutherland, Thomas Meighan's nephew.

"I didn't like him," she said. "All he did was talk about himself and his next picture."

Later she realized the reason; he was terribly excited because of his breaks in pictures and he wanted to tell someone all about it.

Their second meeting was in Florida in 1926, where Bebe was filming *The Palm Beach Girl*. So was Ben. He was wearing a beard for his next picture and he told her that wise-guys kept yanking his beard to see if it was real. Bebe still wasn't impressed by Ben or his beard. They did not meet again for some time.

BEN

9

Like Father, Like Son

Ben was born in Atlanta, Georgia, on 6 February 1901, exactly three weeks after Bebe was born in Dallas, Texas. And there the coincidence of their lives beginning almost at the same time might have ended, "because," Ben would say, "our early backgrounds were entirely different. Unlike Bebe, my parents weren't in the theatre. I wasn't carried on the stage as a baby and I wasn't a child actor. Compared with Bebe I was a late starter. I didn't get my first break in the theatre until I was seventeen. By then Bebe was a 'veteran', but," and he would laugh, "I finally caught up with her!"

There was no reason for his family to think he would become an actor. "My father was a business man. His business was promoting and selling bedroom furniture, including mattresses, and he had plans for me when I left school. Like father, like son, he hoped I would join him in his business and live happily ever after.

"My grandfather had other ideas. He had a factory in Atlanta, making ladies' sunbonnets, and he could see me taking over the factory when I grew up. So the choice between my father and grandfather was mattresses and sunbonnets. That's the way my folks thought — it just didn't work out that way."

German military fanaticism twice influenced Ben's life; first, through his grandparents. They came to America from Leipzig in the 1860s. They left Germany because his grandfather was an outspoken opponent of the fanatical German military regime of that period. So with his wife and children he sailed for America and finally arrived in Atlanta, Georgia, in the deep South where they settled. Grandfather Lyon was an industrious man, and he and his wife were prepared to work hard to achieve a rightful and respected place as American citizens.

At that time Atlanta was *Gone With The Wind* country, a land of plantations and elegant colonial-style houses, a land which gave birth to negro spirituals and smiling, buxom, coloured mammies, epitomized in films and songs many years later. In Atlanta the sun shone almost continuously. Ladies wore silk and cotton crinolines – and sunbonnets. When grandfather Lyon arrived into this warm, sleepy country from the colder climate of Leipzig, he noticed the ladies' sunbonnets.

"I'm going to make sunbonnets," he announced one day to his wife.

She shrugged. "Whatever gave you that idea? All the ladies wear them."

Grandfather smiled mysteriously. "Ah," – he shook a forefinger at her. "But I don't like what I see."

"Meaning . . .?"

"Most of their bonnets look like helmets. They are too plain, not pretty enough. I'll show you."

While he did some drawings, grandmother put on her sunbonnet and looked at herself in a mirror, Yes, it *did* look like a helmet. From then on, she helped her husband to create new designs.

"I shall make you the first one!" he said, "and you shall wear it for everyone to see."

Recalling stories about those days, Ben would say, "Grandfather bought a small plot of land – remember you could buy land for – what? –a few hundred dollars compared with thousands today; and on the plot of land he built a shop, where he and my grandmother worked and lived. He designed the sunbonnets and she made them up. They caught on; from a few dozen, sales increased to hundreds a year, so grandfather pulled down the shop and built a factory. In the end, the sunbonnets sold in other states as well as Georgia – and he produced thousands.

"I can just remember – I was about four – going down to the factory and watching all the people working on rows of sunbonnets. To keep me busy – and with an eye to the future – grandfather used to pay me a few cents to pick up pieces of material from the floor which the cutters dropped. Hoping one day I would go into business, he thought the earlier I learnt the better!"

But with changing times in the new century and with a new woman's outlook emerging, the sunbonnet crowning demure ringlets gradually gave way to more emancipated hair styles and hats. The factory disappeared and with it grandfather's hopes that one day Ben might take it over. The sunbonnet dream faded – to die altogether when grandfather died. However, there was his father's ambition for Ben – to join *him* in selling bedroom furniture and mattresses. Styles would change, but anyone going into that sort of business would have an assured future.

It simply didn't work out that way.

The second time German military fanaticism influenced Ben's life was in World War II, when he and Bebe decided to stay in Britain instead of returning to America on the outbreak of war with Nazi Germany. But that is a later story.

10

" When Do I Go On? "

Ben was the fourth child of Alvine and Benjamin Lyon. Theirs had been a romantic, runaway marriage, reminiscent of an often told story of the Victorian days when fathers were the head of the house and had more than a say in whom their daughters would marry. Young Benjamin Lyon and two of his friends had a three-piece band. Benjamin was the pianist. They played at dances and local affairs, making a good if somewhat sporadic living. One night, at a dance at which the band was playing, he met Alvine. She was seventeen. He was a little older. They fell in love, but nobody took the young pianist and Alvine seriously until one day, dressed in his best suit, Benjamin called on her father by appointment and asked his permission to marry Alvine. Her father exploded, "No!" – and in best Victorian tradition, he told his daughter's suitor never to darken his door again. So Alvine and Benjamin eloped.

Young Benjamin soon proved he was no erstwhile pianist, prepared to support his wife and family on the uncertain earnings of a three-piece band. He went into the business of promoting and selling bedroom suites, smothering his musical talents under mattresses, and built himself quite a business.

Benjamin and Alvine settled down to married life. Their first three children were two girls, Josephine and Robertine; and a boy, Edwin. Josephine was ten, Robertine nine, and Edwin seven years old when Ben was born. He was named Benjamin after his father, but the name was shortened to Ben to avoid the confusion of having two Benjamins in the family. Josephine and Robertine enjoyed 'mothering' the new baby; Edwin wasn't so interested. Ben was born into an adult and fast growing up household. As the novelty wore off of having a much younger brother, Ben can remember feeling outside the things he could not share with his sisters and brother.

They were a musical family. His father's talents as a pianist were never quite smothered by mattresses and his mother had a sweet singing voice. Ben remembers countless musical evenings round the piano, everybody taking it in turns to sing solos and duets. "My grandparents or friends came over. Sometimes I was allowed to stay up for a while and listen, but mostly I was in bed before the musical evenings began. I would listen to it all until I fell asleep. I had no idea how to go about it, but I wanted to be part of the applause after my mother or sisters sang or my father played a solo piece. I wanted them to applaud me.

"At other times when my sisters were learning a new song – Robertine playing the piano, Josephine singing – I would try to join in. They would be patient with me for a while, but I can't tell you the number of times I was sent out on the porch to eat ice cream to get me out of the way. Edwin? He liked messing about with tools, making things, so I used to try messing around like him, often ending up by hitting my thumb with a hammer. Then I'd start to howl; to stop me howling, more ice cream."

Ben was five years old when the family moved to Baltimore. Baltimore proved to be everything the family hoped it would be. Benjamin's business flourished; Edwin and the girls found new friends at school; they were soon in the social whirl of dances to which Edwin escorted his sisters; there were concerts and amateur theatricals in which the girls took part. When they weren't at school or studying, it seemed the house was filled with music and rehearsing. On the fringe of these activities, Ben longed to be part of it all. At last the opportunity came. Josephine was asked to sing in a charity concert at the Maryland Theatre. It was quite an event with talented young people of Baltimore taking part. Josephine chose a popular song, 'Won't You Be My Baby Boy?' To build it into a presentation, she decided that at the end of the song she would leave the stage, return to sing a reprise of the chorus and bring Ben on with her, singing the chorus to him.

Everyone thought this was a lovely idea. Ben was taken shopping and rigged out in a smart new white sailor suit and hat. Sailor suits were in fashion for small boys. Edward VII was the sailor King of the British Empire, and this was a great era of the sea in Britain and America.

For weeks before the concert the song was rehearsed at home until Ben's entrance and his reaction to Josephine singing to him was perfect. At last the night arrived. The theatre was packed. Just before Josephine went on, Robertine took Ben into the wings. He stood wide-eyed with excitement, watching all the comings and goings, not daring to move an inch in his immaculate white sailor suit. He had never been in the wings of a theatre, and from his vantage point the stage stretched away big and shining in lights to the wings on the other side, but he had no feeling of stage fright. The act before Josephine's finished. For the first time he heard applause from the stage side of the footlights, as the performers took their curtain calls. Josephine's entrance was on the other side of the stage from where Ben waited. There she was, standing in the wings, all shining in her new satin dress and a rose in her hair. Then suddenly she was on stage and the orchestra struck up the opening bars of 'Won't You Be My Baby Boy?' At the end of the song she got tremendous applause. Bouquets were handed up from friends and admirers. Josephine curtsied over and over again before the final curtain and, surprised by the volume of applause, she left the stage. Ben still stood glued to the floor on his side of the wings. Suddenly he was swept away – and before he knew what was happening, the family was on a tramcar going home. So far he had been perfectly quiet. He was too young to understand how these things worked. Maybe everything had been changed and the family was taking a ride before the encore or taking all those flowers home before the scene Josephine had rehearsed with him. Everybody seemed to be talking at once.

"Wasn't Josephine just wonderful!"

"Mama, Daddy — look at these flowers!"

Ben sat beside his father and opposite his mother and sisters. His father, clutching some of the flowers, looked down at Ben and smiled. "Okay son?" Ben nodded. The ribbon floating down from the back of his sailor hat swayed slightly to and fro with the motion of the tramcar. Suddenly he climbed down from his seat, crossed to his mother and leaned on her knee. "Mama," he asked, "when do I go on?"

11

Boy Actor

Eight years on to 1916. Ben was now fifteen and in this year his parents moved to New York. World War I was about midway through, but at fifteen the war made little impact on him. It was a long way off in Europe. America did not come into it until 1917. Movies, though, had made great strides and newsreels of the fighting were shown in cinemas.

"I can remember being thrilled when we arrived in New York. It wasn't, of course, anything like it is today. Horse-drawn vehicles mingled with motor cars and streets were still lit by gas, but it had all the *feel* of a great city — bustling and alive. I was sent to High School to complete my studies and I guess my parents hoped I would go on to University, but I didn't." Ben didn't go to University because the move to New York changed the whole course of his life.

Movies were the 'in' thing. Names like Charlie Chaplin, Bill Hart, the cowboy star, Wallace Reid, Mary Pickford, Harold

Lloyd and Bebe Daniels were becoming household names.

New York was as much a centre of film-making as California, three thousand miles away. It remained so for many years with film studios springing up and going out of business. But others remained and these turned out some outstanding productions. Movies were also being made at Fort Lee, New Jersey, then the Hollywood of the East. Here, Pearl White made many of her suspense serials, tied hand and foot to a railway track with an express train approaching; on cliff tops; or in a saw mill about to be sawn in half. At the crucial moment, with the audience nearly leaping out of its seats to save her – 'To be continued' came up on the screen. People went week after week to see her rescued just in time by the hero only to face another terror the following week. Most famous of these serials was *The Perils of Pauline*.

To sixteen-year-old Ben and his contemporaries, movies were their 'scene'. Heroes and heroines of the silver screen were their pin-ups.

One New York studio was 'The Famous Players'. Ben passed the studio every day to and from school. All his boyhood dreams of becoming an actor seemed to lie behind its doors.

"Believe me," he would say, "although I used to imagine myself as a Bill Hart or Wallace Reid, it took a lot of courage for me to go through those doors. I wasn't really a brash kid. When it came to the crunch I was nervous."

One day on his way home from school he found enough courage, walked into the studio and knocked on a door labelled 'Casting Office'.

"Come in," it was a woman's voice. Ben opened the door and walked in. The woman sat behind a desk covered with papers. She eyed the schoolboy carrying his books strapped together. Ben shifted from one foot to the other. For a few seconds he was tongue-tied. He stood erect and stiff, hoping he looked tall and impressive.

"Well?" The woman waited.

"I want to get into pictures. How do I go about it please?"

The woman took off her spectacles and her glance swept over the books Ben was carrying; then over Ben himself. The glance conveyed that she had heard it all a hundred times before. Ben felt he was shrinking – not nearly as tall as he really was, certainly not impressive. His mouth had gone dry and his voice sounded high-pitched to him. The woman smiled disconcertingly, but she said kindly enough, "I'll give you a form to fill in." She put on her spectacles, opened a drawer in the desk, took out a form and handed it to him. "Send this back to us with some photographs of yourself."

So he *had* made an impression! Her next comment wasn't so good. "We can't promise anything – there's no work right now." Ben took the form saying, "Thank you," and started to exit.

In later years he said, "She must have handed out dozens of those forms to movie-struck kids like myself. I shall never forget her – Miss Rose was her name. I don't think I made the slightest impression on her, and if I'd left the office that would have been the end of my movie-struck dreams."

As luck would have it, just as Ben was going, an inner door opened and a stocky man strode in. He stopped and looked at Ben for an interminable few seconds. Ben stood rooted, not knowing whether to stay or go. Suddenly the man waved a hand at him and said to Miss Rose, "He's fine." Miss Rose nodded and the man beckoned Ben. "Follow me." Leaving his books and the form with Miss Rose, he followed the man to a dressing room.

Ben looked round. The dressing room seemed to be full of dwarfs. Someone handed him a stick of yellow greasepaint. Yellow was the colour they used for film make-up. He stood there, holding the stick and looking at it. If only Josephine was here, he thought, she'd know what to do. He felt all eyes turn towards him. He had no idea how to put on the make-up and everyone in the dressing room knew it. Suddenly one of the dwarfs hopped on a stool and took the greasepaint from him. "Here kid – I'll do it."

"I learnt another first lesson from that," said Ben. "People in show business help each other. That dwarf knew I hadn't a clue about make-up, so he did it for me."

"What's the film?" Ben asked the dwarf.

"*Snow White*," the dwarf replied.

Ben was baffled. How could they be casting him as a dwarf? He was too tall. But he dare not ask questions. They knew what they were doing, so he let his imagination run away as the dwarf made him up. Perhaps they saw him as the prince? No, not the prince. Perhaps a courtier . . . something important anyway. The dwarf broke in on his thoughts. "You're done." He hopped down off the stool, stepped back and looked up at Ben. "You look fine."

Ben managed a "Thanks", not daring to move a muscle of his face for fear of spoiling the make-up as someone took him into the studio. "It was a huge barn of a place," he said. "In one corner a company was making a movie; another company was busy in another corner. They could make all the noise they wanted. It couldn't affect the film.

"The director stood me in front of a black velvet curtain facing a camera. Suddenly I was flooded in light. The director told me, 'When I say camera! . . . action! . . . smile . . . I want you to smile, understand?' I nodded. 'Okay,' and he disappeared into the blackness beyond the lights.

"I heard him shout, 'Camera' . . . action! . . . *SMILE!*'

"I hadn't the faintest idea how to smile when I was told to, and it must have been the silliest grin you've ever seen. Then the director's voice again, '*CUT!*' As suddenly as the lights had come on they were switched off. Someone took my arm and said, 'Thanks son, you were okay' — and I was led away from the black velvet curtain. I was handed on to a young woman carrying a script. She smiled, 'Can you find your way to the dressing room, and Miss Rose will give you a pay slip.'

"Back in the dressing room the same dwarf helped me take off the make-up.

" 'How did it go, kid?' he asked.

" 'Fine — and thanks a lot.' Then I was back in Miss Rose's office. I was paid five dollars — about £2 in those days — a lot of money for a few seconds filming."

Up to now Ben had said very little. He was too awed by the whole thing. He couldn't believe it was so easy to get into films. At last he found his tongue.

"What am I in *Snow White*?" he asked Miss Rose.

"Oh, you're not in *Snow White* — you're in *The Travelling Salesmen*."

She knew he was touched with the charisma of it all and

73

would probably never do anything else, but she took the trouble to tell him about the film. It was the story of some salesmen who couldn't get home for Christmas, so dejectedly they played cards in an hotel room on Christmas Day.

"As the salesmen hold their cards fanwise," she explained, "the diamonds, hearts, clubs and spades dissolve into the faces of their wives and children . . . you're one of the children. I won't tell you any more. Go and see it for yourself."

Ben asked, "Shall I call in again?"

Miss Rose shook her head. "We'll call you if we want you."

Ben was to hear that phrase many times in the years ahead. "Don't call us – we'll call you." Too often it means – forget it.

"I couldn't dash home fast enough to tell my mother how I'd broken into pictures. She listened patiently. My father was away travelling at the time. I thought he'd be tickled pink that I was in a film called *The Travelling Salesmen*, so I wrote him. Instead of being pleased, he wrote back to mother forbidding me ever to take part again in such a 'disgraceful escapade'."

But Ben was badly bitten by the acting bug. His mother realized this. When *The Travelling Salesmen* was released – films were made quickly in those days so it soon came out – he and his mother went to see it about eight times.

"My flash on and off the screen seemed to get shorter each time," Ben would laugh. After seeing it for the last time before the cinema changed its programme, he thought of Miss Rose's words, "We'll call you if we want you." For weeks he waited for a call. It never came.

Now he had the choice: to leave school and try to get into movies. Persuaded by his mother, his father agreed to let him try. "I'll give you a year," he said.

For the next few days, Ben walked on clouds. The dreamer always at his elbow nudged him along.

He recalls, "My father didn't want to see me fail or starve. So he said he would match what I earned. If I made, say, twenty dollars he would give me twenty dollars. I got work in the Pearl White serials at Fort Lee – as an extra with dozens

74

of other extras in crowd scenes. This didn't last long and soon I was going the rounds of agents. I had longer periods of unemployment than employment, and my father waited for me to give up the whole idea."

Ben made friends at Fort Lee, among them Norma Shearer. She, like him, was then unknown and was going the rounds of agents' offices. "There was never any romance between us, we were two kids trying to get a break in movies. Norma succeeded long before I did."

Ben went on for a year until he was seventeen, getting nowhere, and the time his father had given him to make good in movies was almost up. So he pretended he was getting along well, even though he had to pay rent for his room as well as buy food — and he had no work. One evening, he wandered along Broadway. It was now 1918. The war in Europe was over. All around him, people were celebrating victory. Theatres were booming. Surely someone, somewhere, wanted him. He couldn't face the thought of becoming a salesman in his father's business. In later years, looking back, he would produce a write-up which said, "In 1918 Ben Lyon temporarily gave up film work." He would laugh. "The truth was — film work gave up me." It was during that walk along Broadway that he decided to try the theatre.

12

The Boy From Baltimore

Seventeen. Ben's age and the title of the Booth Tarkington play in which he got his first break as a juvenile lead. Ben portrayed a romantic and dashing character called George Crooper, and he was paid thirty-five dollars a week.

"How I ever got the part, I never knew," Ben would recall. "I really didn't know how to act; I only thought I did, but when you're seventeen you can get away with mostly anything. Somehow I convinced the management that I *could* act. I'd had no conventional training – what I knew I had picked up by watching people in the theatre and movies. It's nothing new for a kid to say, 'I want to be an actor' and then it fizzles out, but with me it stuck. *Seventeen* ran in New York for two years, then went on tour. We toured parts of America and Canada. I learned a lot from that tour, but I still didn't learn to *act*. I must have been the biggest ham that ever walked on any stage. I thought the thing to do was to project my voice loudly. A lot of young actors make that mistake. Once I was on stage, I found myself listening, fascinated, to my own voice, not using it. Also I assumed a slight swagger." Ben would laugh. "I thought I was great. How I got away with it, I don't know, but the play was a success and I was banking money when the run of *Seventeen* finished."

Ben went straight into another play, *The Wonderful Thing* at two hundred dollars a week, playing opposite Jeanne Eagles, a Broadway star of those days.

"Jeanne was a lovely person," Ben recalls, "and I can't imagine now how she put up with my mannerisms and my voice!"

With Ben's early upbringing in Atlanta, Georgia, and because his parents never lost the soft drawl and phrases of the deep South, Ben inherited these. It took him a long time to lose phrases like, "how are y'awl (you all) honey chil' " with an upward inflection. When he first went into the theatre, he would say things like, "close the winder". Words like 'window' were pronounced more like 'winder', or 'yellow' more like 'yeller'. So when he had a line "close the window", he kept saying, "close the winder". The director interrupted him, "Ben it's not *winder*, it's *window* – close the wind*ow*."

"That's what I'm saying," Ben replied, "close the winder. Finally I got it."

After *The Wonderful Thing* closed, Ben was out of work for six months. Once again, he went from agent to agent and was told, "don't call us, we'll call you". Finally he went back to films and a company called Vitagraph gave him a job in a film, *The Heart of Maryland*. This time he was in a supporting role which billed his name and gave him a screen credit.

In Ben's seesaw existence, up one day and down the next, the same pattern repeated itself. After *The Heart of Maryland*, no more work; no more film offers. So back to the stage in a minor role in a play, *Three Live Ghosts*. When this closed he was offered the lead on tour in another play, *Sun Up*. One evening at the end of a performance word went round the cast, "We're booked for Broadway!" Magical words for a hard-working cast on tour. They celebrated with a bumper supper, spending more than they could really afford. Came the last night of the tour and the final curtain. As Ben took his bow with the cast, then alone as the lead, he thought, "Next time I do this, it will be on a Broadway stage." He bowed low and long to the small-town audience as the curtain came down for the last time.

As the cast disappeared into the wings towards their dressing rooms, leaving the stage with that momentous emptiness before the stage hands start dismantling scenery and clearing away props, the director, waiting backstage, stopped Ben and drew him into a corner.

"We're going to New York tomorrow," he began.

Ben smiled broadly. "I know."

"We open on Broadway in two weeks, and Ben . . ." Ben waited, still smiling. " . . . I'd better tell you now. You won't be playing the lead on Broadway. We've had to choose another actor."

Ben's smile disappeared as if an unseen hand had wiped it from his face. He managed a strangled, "Why?"

"I'm afriad your performance isn't good enough . . . Sorry."

In a shaky voice Ben asked, "Do the others know?"

The director shook his head. "Not yet — they won't until we get to New York. But don't worry, you'll be okay." It was a trite remark meant to help, but it didn't.

The journey back to New York was miserable. Ben kept up a pretence that he was thrilled with the prospect of Broadway, but the director's words kept running through his mind. "Your performance isn't good enough."

At last he accepted that he could *not* act and he must stop pretending to himself that he knew it all. Back in New York he sought out people who could give him advice. He went to cafés and restaurants frequented by film and theatre people; not stars, but actors and actresses who made a good living out of supporting roles and who knew the business backwards. He asked them, "What can I do?". Without exception they told him, "Join a good stock company. Learn the business from the bottom." If his inner voice said incredibly, "Begin again at the bottom!", he was sensible enough now to toss out the voice. He joined the then famous Jessie Bonstell Stock Company. His salary, twenty-five dollars a week; a massive landslide from the two hundred dollars a week he had earned in *The Wonderful Thing* playing opposite Jeanne Eagles.

"Jessie Bonstell was responsible for making many stars who joined her company," Ben would say. "As I recall, about sixty to seventy per cent of the youngsters who joined her made it to the top, including people like Catherine Cornell and Anne Harding. Remember I was still only twenty, so there was plenty of time."

He stayed with the company for two years, touring places like Buffalo, Rhode Island, Providence. He listened and learned. He was never too big to play a small part and he worked hard. The company put on a new play each week, so while the current production was running the cast were learning and rehearsing their parts for the next week's performance. A player could have anything up to a hundred pages of a new play to learn while they were acting in the current play.

When the stage was free from rehearsals, Jessie Bonstell took her youngsters one by one and put them through their paces. Today it was Ben's turn. Sitting in the stalls with Ben on stage, Jessie said, "I want you to go through your speech in Scene Two." He started. After a while she called, "Stop!"

He came down to the footlights and crouched to listen attentively to what she would say.

"I know exactly what you're doing," said Jessie. "You *think* you are projecting your voice. So you are – but you're listening to it, aren't you? It won't do."

Ben's heart sank. Was she going to say he wasn't good

enough? From his expression, Jessie sensed what he was thinking.

"Don't worry about it. We can cure it, but I must remind you – the theatre is *communicating* to the audience. You've got to make them *feel* what you are feeling. Understand?"

"Jessie was blunt and to the point," Ben recalls, "but she never made you feel ridiculous or inferior. I lapped up everything she said."

At the end of two years, he felt able to leave the security of Jessie Bonstell's stock company and try his luck again in New York. Jessie encouraged him to go. He was now twenty-two – experienced and far more mature. Word had gone ahead of him that he was a promising young actor. This he attributed to Jessie. She had wanted to know where he would be staying. Soon after he arrived in New York the tables were completely turned. Instead of Ben knocking on agents' doors, an agent called him and offered him the lead of what was later to be the Broadway success *Mary the Third*. In this he would play with Louise Huff, a star of the 1920s. The story of *Mary the Third* covered three generations of a girl's life. The play called for two male leads. Ben played one opposite Louise Huff and another actor, as unknown then as Ben, played the other male lead – Humphrey Bogart, 'Bogey' to his friends.

"Bogey and I got on fine," Ben would recall, "but he wasn't happy with his part. For one thing, he had to wear a blonde wig which he hated. We both had dark hair and were about the same height and build. So the producer, Rachel Crothers – she wrote the play – insisted that one of us must be blonde."

Mary the Third opened in Connecticut, and before the opening night Ben and Humphrey Bogart tried to persuade Rachel to drop the idea of the blonde wig. She waved their arguments aside. "You've got to think of the gallery. You look too much alike. I can't have two leads with dark hair."

"But we don't talk alike," said Ben.

"Ben could wear a dark suit and I can wear a light suit," Humphrey Bogart suggested.

Rachel would not listen. Bogey had to wear the blonde wig. The result: he was unhappy in the part, he played it badly, and the critics panned him.

One night, after only a few performances, Ben was taking off his make-up in his dressing room. The door opened and Bogey looked in.

"Got a minute?" he asked Ben.

"Sure," said Ben, "come on in."

Bogey closed the door behind him and sat down. He looked unhappy.

"What's on your mind?" Ben asked.

"I'm leaving." Bogey smiled wryly, "or to be more exact, Rachel has asked me to go."

"Oh no!"

"Oh yes! She doesn't like the way I'm playing the part. It's that darned wig. She was nice about it, but she's right, Ben. I'll mess up the whole thing for everybody."

"But Bogey, what are you going to do?"

Bogey shrugged, the shrug that became famous in later years. "I don't know yet — but I won't wear that wig."

Ben shook his head. He liked Bogey and he was worried. "Pity," he said, "you're throwing away a good chance."

As it turned out, it was Rachel Crothers who threw away a good chance. The next thing Ben heard about Humphrey Bogart was that he was a great success in *The Petrified Forest*.

"The beginning of his brilliant career," said Ben later. "Was I pleased for him!"

While this was happening the film industry was growing fast. Films were still being made at Fort Lee and one of the producers there was Sam Goldwyn. Contrary to popular belief, certain producers and directors did not start in Hollywood, Sam Goldwyn among them. They went there later and helped to make Hollywood the great film centre it finally became. Like all producers, Sam Goldwyn went to the theatre, partly because he enjoyed it and also to look for talent. One evening he went to see *Mary the Third*. Recalling that evening, Ben said, "Sam Goldwyn was already a big name in the film world. If I'd known he was out front, I would probably have given my worst performance out of sheer nerves."

Fortunately he didn't know. "The next morning I had a call from my agent, Eddie Small."

"Sam Goldwyn wants to see you," Eddie said to a speechless Ben. "He was at the theatre last night and was impressed by you. You'd better come over so I can give you a bit of advice."

The advice was about money and the kind of offer Eddie Small knew from experience Sam Goldwyn would make.

"He'll offer you one picture. You must say you'll do at least three in a row. Understood? And you'll ask for six hundred dollars a week. He'll say three hundred. You'll settle for four hundred."

A bemused Ben protested, "I can't dictate that way to Sam Goldwyn."

"You can and you will," replied Eddie. He took Ben's arm and ushered him through the door. "Come back when you've made the deal."

Sam Goldwyn was in the hall of his apartment putting on his hat and coat when Ben arrived. "I'm going out," he said, "and I'm in a hurry. Care to walk with me?"

They walked along the select and sedate Park Avenue, silently at first. "Sam Goldwyn set a terrific pace," said Ben. "I wondered afterwards if that was the way he did things. After all, it's difficult to argue with a man you're trying to keep up with along a busy avenue and dodge people at the same time."

Sam Goldwyn glanced sideways at Ben. "Eddie Small has told you – I want you in my next picture, *Potash and Perlmutter*. You'll be the juvenile lead. I'm starting shooting soon."

"Yes sir! . . . Mr. Goldwyn . . . thank you . . ." Ben stepped on one side to allow two ladies to pass. Sam Goldwyn forged ahead. Ben hurried to catch up.

"When do you start shooting Mr. Goldwyn?"

"In a few days."

"I'm in 'Mary the Third' . . ."

"I know. I saw you last night."

Ben lost ground again. Catching up, he plucked up all his courage and repeated what Eddie Small had told him.

"I couldn't do just one picture . . . If it were three in a row of course . . ."

Sam Goldwyn shook his head. His pace quickened even more. "Can't offer you that. I do one picture at a time.

You'll suit *Potash and Perlmutter* fine. Want it?"

Ben thought fast. Was Eddie right? Dare he say six hundred dollars? What had he to lose? If Sam Goldwyn said "no", he could go on in *Mary the Third*. Another sidestep – another catching up. "For six hundred dollars a week, I'll do it,' he blurted at Sam Goldwyn.

Sam Goldwyn didn't stop and he didn't change his expression. "I'll give you three hundred dollars," he countered. Ben couldn't believe his ears. It was just as Eddie had predicted. Okay, he'd carry the whole thing through. "Five hundred dollars!" he almost shouted.

In that select avenue, people turned to look at these two, rushing along, clipping hundreds of dollars at each other.

"Four hundred – and it's settled!"

Ben tripped on the kerb, stubbing his toe as they crossed an intersection. He stopped. A sharp pain ran through his foot.

"I'll contact Eddie Small," was Sam Goldwyn's final remark as he strode on. Ben stood and watched him until he disappeared. Goldwyn did not look back. From that meeting, Ben was not to look back for a long time. Sam Goldwyn signed him to play the juvenile lead in *Potash and Perlmutter*. Eddie Small was jubilant. "I knew you could do it," he said.

Ben smiled broadly. "I almost broke my toe."

Eddie looked puzzled, but Ben didn't explain. In later years he often recalled the famous Sam Goldwyn cryptic comment if someone had something to say: "If you've got a message, use Western Union!"

Potash and Perlmutter was a success. When shooting finished, Ben asked Eddie Small, "What next?"

"You're going to Hollywood," he replied.

Ben didn't argue. After the Sam Goldwyn episode he trusted Eddie's judgement. Everyone in the business knew that Hollywood was fast becoming associated with movies. He had saved enough money to take the chance and pay his way. If he didn't succeed, he could always come back to New York.

"Heck," said Eddie. "What kind of talk is that? Not succeeding! Sure you'll succeed!"

The boy from Baltimore was on his way.

13

And So To Hollywood

The year, 1923. Ben was twenty-two years old when he set out from New York to Los Angeles and Hollywood, a journey of three thousand miles by train across America from east to west. He had seen quite a bit of America on tour, but he had never been as far west as California. As the train carried him across that vast continent he had time to reflect that this had been the way of those early migrants who had gone in search of gold. He had time to reflect that it had taken but a short fifty years of railroad building to link the Atlantic coast with the Pacific, yet echoes of the old wagon trains crossing the plains still seemed to linger. In those days, "Go west, young man" was no idle piece of advice to some restless young man from the east.

When he settled down on the west coast, Ben would go to places the Spaniards had named after saints when they were in California, places that would one day have a far greater meaning for him than just names: Santa Monica, where in the years to come he and Bebe would have their home; Santa Barbara, where they would spend their honeymoon. Later, when their daughter was born she would be named Barbara.

The Spanish influence remained in the names of Los Angeles (The Angels) and San Francisco (St Francis). San Francisco, Ben would discover, was one of the most beautiful coastal cities in California.

When he arrived in Hollywood, he rented a bungalow with a friend and co-actor, Boyce Coon. "I had no idea whether I would get film work," he would say. "If not, it would be a good vacation." He had only been there a few days when the phone rang.

"Hullo Ben . . . Ben Lyon?"

"Yes, who is it?"

"I'm John McCormick. I've heard from Eddie Small about you. I'm calling from First National Studios. We've seen *Potash and Perlmutter* and we'd like to see *you*. Care to come over?"

Ben went over right away and was offered a part in a film *Painted People* with Coleen Moore. He hadn't expected things to happen this fast, and he attributed a great deal of it to those two years with the Jessie Bonstell company. In his heart he always thanked Jessie and he never forgot her. One thing he did not realize when he arrived in California was that actors and actresses, hearing reports that Hollywood was becoming a kind of Mecca in which everyone was growing rich, were flowing into Los Angeles. "There was a boom, certainly, but the boom had its repercussions. It was one of the most disturbing things at that time to see the amount of unemployment. So I was lucky."

Painted People led to more films. One of the stories Ben told to friends in England many years later was his audition for *Ben Hur*, to be made by Metro-Goldwyn-Mayer.

"Someone got the idea that I would make a good Ben Hur. Studios were then making really spectacular films and at M-G-M they said, 'Okay, test him.' In some scenes I would be filmed with a bare chest, so I stripped down to the waist for the test. At that time I was slim – thin, I guess you'd say. Anyway, you could count my ribs, no muscles. Someone made a crack about me looking like a greyhound; that just about summed it up. I looked as if I'd come out of trap three! But they still seemed to want me, so they sent for a make-up man and he *painted* muscles on me. By the time he'd finished, I looked like a weight-lifter or a wrestler, bulging with muscles. Then they sprayed me with oil so that the muscles shone and would stand out under the lights. Well, there we were, waiting for the test. Someone shouted, 'Lights!' and on went a battery of them, generating heat on to me. Within seconds the oil started running. It trickled down my body – and my muscles gradually trickled down into my pants. That was the end of Ben Hur for me – Ramon Navarro got the part." But other films followed and Ben was on the road to stardom.

It would be some time, though, before he met Bebe Daniels. They worked in different studios. It was only likely that he might bump into her at a party, although neither of them were great party-goers. Bebe was too busy making films and Ben too eager to build a career. They had their own friends, "and," said Ben, "there was no reason why Bebe, already an established star, should seek out Ben Lyon."

Their first two meetings are told in Bebe's story.

Came the third chance meeting in New York at a supper dance at the Ritz Carlton Hotel. Ben was escorting Marilyn Miller. "We were dancing and suddenly we came face to face with Bebe and Jack Pickford (Mary Pickford's brother) dancing together. We all stopped and said 'hullo'. After the dance we sat down at our own tables and there it might have ended, but it was strange ... I wasn't thinking about Bebe — as a matter of fact I was very fond of Marilyn — but if I glanced up or across the floor, I looked at Bebe. It was something magnetic. I can't explain. She and Jack were completely engrossed with each other and I'm sure Bebe didn't glance my way once."

In 1924 Ben co-starred with Pola Negri in *Lily of the Dust*, and with Barbara La Marr in *The White Moth*. In the same year he went to New York for Paramount to co-star with Gloria Swanson in *Wages of Virtue*. Back to Hollywood and more films, including *Hell's Angels*.

Bebe was back in Hollywood from New York. She and Ben met again at a bridge party. Bebe was an expert bridge player — Ben was not. "However," he said, "when Bebe and two other experts wanted a fourth, I volunteered! I was drawn with Bebe. By a fluke I got through the first hand and Bebe smiled at me. But the second hand — I made a mess of it. Everybody laughed about it, but I could see by Bebe's expression she really didn't think it was funny at all. Whatever I did, I couldn't get anywhere with her, yet something kept telling me — go on trying!

"My next chance was at a restaurant where I went one evening for dinner. And there was Bebe having dinner with Gary Cooper. Now what, I thought, can I do to get her to ask me to join them? Well, I walked backwards and forwards past their table several times, but they were so busy talking they didn't even see me. So I tipped the waiter to let me take his place. As I served Bebe's soup I stuck my thumb in it. The soup was hot and it creased my thumb, but I didn't care.

"I waited for some reaction. Nothing happened! Neither Bebe nor Gary noticed what I had done. I didn't let Bebe eat the soup — I stopped her. She looked up, recognized me, and I told her what I had done. She laughed, so did Gary, but I don't think either of them thought it was funny. I *wasn't* invited to join them. Exit me again.

"What next? We met again at the Coconut Grove, and at least this time Bebe let me drive her home."

Either by accident or design, Ben turned up wherever Bebe happened to be. On another occasion he drove her home after she had been swimming. He asked her to have dinner with him that night. She was sorry, she said, she couldn't. She was having dinner with Johnny Weismuller (Hollywood's Tarzan). Ben threatened if she didn't break the date he would turn her out of the car on Sunset Boulevard in her swimsuit and robe. He was getting masterful. She broke the date with Johnny Weismuller.

At that time flying was becoming a popular occupation and Ben could talk with authority about it. One day when he met Bebe at a friend's house, he talked with such enthusiasm about the future of aviation that she listened to him with interest. Suddenly she said, "I'd love to learn to fly."

Ben reacted quickly. "You would?"

Bebe nodded, "Love it."

"Okay, I'll teach you."

"You *will?*"

"Sure."

Before they went home, Ben drew Bebe on one side. "If I teach you to fly, will you do something for me?"

Bebe raised her eyebrows, looking at him questioningly. She didn't answer.

Ben smiled. "Will you teach me to play bridge?"

Remembering the night of the bridge party, Bebe laughed outright. "All right," she agreed.

It all began to fall into place. They enjoyed each other's company. Ben taught Bebe to fly. She became a proficient pilot and took her pilot's licence.

"But," she said, "everyone used to call me 'Wing Low the Chinese pilot' because I always flew with my left wing down." Watching her from the ground or sitting behind her in the aeroplane, Ben could never correct this and get Bebe to fly the plane straight. Neither could Roscoe Turner, Ben's pilot friend, who also took a hand in Bebe's lessons.

And Bebe taught Ben to play bridge.

After Bebe and Ben were married, they owned their own aeroplane, a Stinson.

"One day," Ben recalls, "Little Mother said she would like to 'go flying.' At first I was a little nervous about taking her up — she was getting on in years — so I asked Bebe what she thought.

"Sure," said Bebe, "take her — she'll love it."

"So I did — and you know something? When she was up she didn't want to come down. And when she was down she wanted to go up again! Of course I didn't do any stunt flying with her, although one day in that lovely accent of hers, she said, 'Why do you not loop-a da loop-a with me?' She got mad at me because I wouldn't do it. She was a great Little Mother!"

By 1929, Germany had made great strides in the film industry. Ben was asked if he would like to make a film there. This was not only an opportunity for him to go to Europe, but it gave him an opportunity to take his mother and sisters for the first time.

The German picture was not yet due to start, so Ben took his mother and sister on a tour of France, Italy and Switzerland. Finally on to London and his first glimpse of the city that would one day be his home. Back in Berlin he co-starred with Lya Mara in *Dancing Vienna*. It is interesting to note here that Ben was the first Hollywood actor to co-star in a German film. Four weeks later, his part in the film completed, he sailed back to America. Josephine returned to Baltimore and Ben took his mother with him to Hollywood. She had never been there and over the years he had seen too little of her. He had not forgotten what she had done for him when he wanted to go into films. "Now I had the chance to do something for her."

His mother was thrilled. She met stars. Ben took her round the studios. "She had a wonderful time."

14

Hell's Angels

In 1926 millionaire Howard Hughes came to Hollywood from Texas. A brilliant engineer and still only in his twenties, he was the head of the Hughes Tool Company of Houston, Texas. He did not come to Hollywood with any idea of being an actor, although he wanted to get into the motion picture industry. He had a driving ambition: to do something creative in the industry, and behind this lay an unshakeable belief in the future of aviation and air travel. He was an accomplished pilot and flew his own planes everywhere.

His first dream of doing something creative in the film industry could be fulfilled by backing films. As a millionaire he had the money to do this, and he did in fact back two films, *Two Arabian Knights* and *Everybody Acting*, made by a producer named Mickie Neilan. The films showed a profit and this encouraged Howard Hughes to go on. Besides, these films had given him the chance to learn the behind-the-camera side of the business — producing and directing. Now he would turn to something more spectacular, not only in story but in realism.

So with the same producer, Mickie Neilan, the idea of *Hell's Angels* was born. This would fulfill the Howard Hughes dream of chronicling the feats of aviators and an outstanding era in the development of aviation. The subject: World War I and a story that would perpetuate the air battles of the Royal Air Force against German pilots. So began the task of research, of writing the story, coupled with Howard Hughes' insistence on historical realism.

Ben takes up the story in his own words: "Howard never lost control of the Hughes Tool Company and this brought him in a fabulous income which meant he could invest in a film of the magnitude he had in mind. R.A.F. pilots were his heroes. Their daring and exploits in fighting the German air force were an inspiration to him so if he made such a film the actual air battle scenes would have to be filmed in the air, with pilot actors shooting it out in the sky — not on the

Ben.

Ben (centre) with Jean Harlow and James Hall in a scene from
Hell's Angels.

Ben in a sinister moment in *I Cover The Waterfront* with Ernest
Torrence.

Bebe, Ben and Barbara on the beach at Santa Monica, California.

'Hi Gang!' Left to right: Ben, Anna Neagle, Bebe, Vic Oliver, Benny Lee (resident singer in the show). (*B.B.C. Copyright photograph.*)

Bebe and Ben during World War II.

ground with sky and aeroplane back projection being used.

"Writing and intensive research started in the winter of 1926. Finally the story was ready, prepared by Mickie Neilan in conjunction with Joseph Moncure March. With aviation experts Howard toured Europe buying up world-war aircraft, many of these from Britain and Germany, and he shipped them back to America. In the end, it was said that Howard owned more aircraft than anyone, except, of course, governments. I can remember a giant German Gotha and Fokker D-VIIs. From Britain came S.E.-5s, Sopwith Camels, Snipes and a few Avros. If you're a millionaire that's the sort of thing you can afford to do. Over a hundred pilots were signed up, some of America's best-known stunt flyers, and a number of former British and German fighter and bomber pilots. Then Howard built an airfield on a vast plot in San Fernando Valley. He constructed a complete flying field down to the last detail. It was called Caddo Field, named after Caddo Oilfield, which provided some of the profits of the Hughes family. Several miles up the valley Howard leased another airfield and rebuilt this to the exact replica of 'The Jolly Baron's Nest', a term used by British fighter pilots to identify the airfield of Baron von Richthofen, the outstanding German air ace. From 'The Jolly Baron's Nest' the notorious Richthofen Flying Circus took off every morning on their bombing flights. All told, we had a ground crew of 150 men, quite an outfit before a foot of *Hell's Angels* was shot."

The airfields were completed, all the aircraft were moved in, the pilots and ground crews ready to go into action. Ben was already a qualified pilot and Howard Hughes starred him to play opposite James Hall as the other male lead, with Greta Nissen, the Swedish actress, for the romantic interest. As pilots, Ben and James Hall were friends in the film, but rivals for Greta Nissen's affections.

"In October 1927, shooting started," Ben recalls. "By the end of that year, interior sequences alone had cost three hundred and fifty thousand dollars, even more than Howard had budgeted for, and he was still spending at the rate of five thousand dollars a day. It's not likely there will ever be another air picture to beat that record! Nobody, I imagine, wants to break it — or they would be broke!

"And now we started the air sequences, the dog fights between British and German planes. Howard himself directed these in the air. There were dozens of planes in the air, circling, diving, spitting fire from guns. And there were terrifying accidents as well as near accidents. Altogether four pilots were killed in these scenes. Newspapers had banner headlines of narrow escapes. The first pilot to have an accident was returning in formation after a dog fight over the sea. Something went wrong with his plane and he baled out. There was a ground mist and he thought he was still over the sea, but he wasn't. His abandoned plane crashed near Joe Schenck's house on Hollywood Boulevard, and the propellor spun off the plane, crashing into the busy Boulevard. How it missed cars and pedestrians we never knew. The pilot landed beside someone else's swimming pool. The newspapers reported it was my plane and Bebe had a bad half-an-hour or so before she got me on the phone.

"When another plane got into trouble, the mechanic realized it too late. He crashed with the plane and was killed. Two other planes got their wings locked, but fortunately the pilots baled out in time . . . I could go on and on. It wasn't all accidents, of course. Those dozens of planes came through dog fights without trouble and flew back safely in formation to the airfields. The realism Howard Hughes got into those scenes was really great."

Roscoe Turner was one of the pilots. Ben recalled him as a "great guy, huge, husky and gusty, with a winning smile and a quick temper.

"In one scene Howard kept flying round Roscoe signalling him to fly lower and lower. Roscoe's temper flew, he zoomed down, and knocked over a camera – sending the cameraman running for his life! When they landed, Roscoe's huge bulk, even bulkier in all the flying gear, marched over to Howard. He said one word: 'Satisfied?'

"But I suppose one of the highlights was the shooting down of a German Zeppelin in flames. James Hall and I were on the ground and we were filmed running away from the blazing Zeppelin at the back of us. In this scene trick photography was used. If we had been as near to that inferno as it looked, we would have been scorched to death."

At last *Hell's Angels* was finished — after nearly two years of filming. "By this time I was getting rather worried because two years off the screen was a long time. You could be forgotten. But we were mistaken in thinking *Hell's Angels* was finished. It was a silent film — no sound dialogue or anything like that. By then talkies were in and Howard made a big decision — to reshoot all the non-flying sequences with sound dialogue. So we were all re-assembled, except Greta Nissen. She couldn't play in the sound version because of her Swedish accent which wouldn't have fitted the story. Now we had to find another blonde to take her place!

"It so happened that I was wandering through the studios one day and stopped to watch a crowd of extras rehearsing a dancing sequence, and there among the dancers was the girl we were looking for. She was wearing a tight-fitting black satin dress and was blonde! I waited for them to break, then walked over to her.

" 'Would you like to play the lead in *Hell's Angels?*' I asked her. She laughed. 'Don't be ridiculous.'

"I assured her I wasn't being ridiculous and fixed an appointment for her to meet Howard Hughes. At first he wasn't a bit impressed, but he agreed to give her a voice test. The test was arranged that same evening. We rehearsed a scene together for about two hours — then it was shot. The rushes were perfect — her acting, her voice, everything about her, and Howard Hughes signed her up at once. The girl? Jean Harlow."

That was how Ben discovered Jean Harlow. From *Hell's Angels* she went on to make a brilliant film career until she died, tragically, after a serious illness at the age of twenty-seven.

So at last *Hell's Angels* was finished. Louella Parsons, the celebrated Hollywood columnist, described it as "Howard Hughes' two million dollar screen bonfire epic ... with graphic scenes actually shot in the air ... an unprecedented feat of daring and stark realism." It was indeed just that in cinematographic terms of the 1920s. It created a sensation and Louella Parsons wound up her comments by reporting the night "When one of the most publicised pictures ever made unreeled before its première audience in Hollywood."

It all had a sequence. Ben and Howard Hughes became great friends, a friendship that lasted many years with both of them so much a part of the Hollywood scene. Furthermore, they had flying in common; and at one period Ben was the only person Howard Hughes would allow to fly his private planes.

15

Sequel

In the 1920s young aviators were helping to develop civil aviation. The 1914-1918 war had produced its own developments, but these were the begoggled young aviators who took to the air in open cockpit aeroplanes which, compared with a jet take-off today, looked as if they wobbled off the ground. They flew their machines over land, oceans, and mountain ranges where vacuum could suck them down like a vacuum cleaner sucking in a feather, to prove that flying would become a way of life in the future.

In America in the 1920s, Ben Lyon was one of these young aviators. He became civil transport pilot No. 373. The low number shows he was among the first pilots in the United States. Later, he became Second-Lieutenant Benjamin B. Lyon, Jnr., of the 322nd Pursuit Squadron, U.S. Army Air Corps. commissioned in March 1931. Even later he qualified for his British Air Ministry Private Pilot's Licence – No. 5633, which tells any pilot it was still quite a low number, and therefore he was one of the early aviators.

Along with other pilots he helped to popularize flying in America; and the fact that he went through the Army Air Force routine served him in good stead in World War II when he flew on missions over enemy-occupied territory.

Privately, when earthquake tremors hit Los Angeles and other parts of California, he flew back and forth with doctors and nurses and carrying people out of the area, as well as Bebe, Barbara and the household.

Sequel

These were the two faces of Ben Lyon: the handsome young actor making good in films, and the begoggled young airman. He and his contemporaries helped to open up not only civil airways in America, but the air mail service. They started with twin-cockpit mail planes and with a slogan, "Through ice and snow the mail must go."

During World War II he and other actors like Clark Gable, David Niven, James Stewart, and Douglas Fairbanks Jnr. had to live down the label "actors in uniform". They did live it down and were accepted as fighting men.

But in the 1920s there were many years yet to come and much to happen before World War II.

BEBE and BEN

16

The Screen Talks!

A new era began in films. Talkies arrived, heralded as "The Screen Talks!" It is cinema history that in 1927 an amazed world heard Al Jolson not only talk but sing from the screen in *The Jazz Singer*. Up to that point the film had been silent. Then suddenly came his voice speaking, followed by his singing the song 'Mammy'. This was sung with such fervour that it moved the cinema-going public not only to tears but to excited conjecture of – what next? More talkies followed; at first like *The Jazz Singer* they were part silent, part sound. The change-over from silent films to talkies was revolutionary yet slow. Like all innovations which threatened to sweep away old orders the 'in' people, in this case silent-film makers, did not accept that voices coming from the screen would continue. Pictures, yes. Voices, no. For one thing it would be too costly financially. So the silent-film makers went on making their films, convinced that talkies would destroy themselves. How could sets be made sound-proof? How could location noises be erased? How could thousands of cinemas be equipped with new apparatus? But men who saw the future of sound on film were convinced that talkies would succeed. One of these, Bebe's second cousin Dr Lee de Forest, had put sound on film in 1922. Talkies, though, did not grow without teething troubles and growing pains. Sound *was* a problem: how to keep out the noise of a whirring camera; how to balance, for instance, voices of people eating at a table against the rattle of china and cutlery.

"For a dinner scene," Ben would explain, "they would bore a hole in the middle of the table and put the microphone under the hole so it wasn't seen – hiding the hole with flowers; but, and this was the problem, the china and cutlery were nearer the microphone than the people sitting at the table. So they had to find a way of getting rid of loud clatter of china and cutlery almost drowning the voices. They did in the end, but the headaches and re-takes!"

Outside locations were another problem; how to muffle

noises, like too many birds singing. They often had to wait for birds to stop singing. Bebe experienced this in an exterior scene of *Rio Rita*. A humming bird, undetected by the technicians, chose to sit beside the microphone during her song. When the rushes were shown, there was more humming bird than Bebe. The entire scene had to be shot again.

Bumps, strange whistling and hissing noises invaded sound tracks, muffling the human voice.

Herbert Wilcox, a leading British film producer/director, recalls some of the difficulties of those days. Herbert Wilcox made the fifth talkie in Hollywood — *Black Waters*.

"Early sound equipment was big and clumsy. Cameras and their operators were shut in glass sound-proof booths to keep out the noise of the camera. Tracking the booths into shots was difficult enough; sometimes the operators nearly suffocated. Then the booth would get in the way of the microphone hanging above the heads of the actors; microphones got into pictures; arguments developed between the technicians.

"Directors wanted actors to move and talk, not stand still; they wanted action with dialogue and this created more difficulties with camera and microphone. In the early days a microphone would be hidden in a massive vase of flowers and the actor was 'anchored' to the vase. When we see early talkies with someone talking or singing beside a vase of flowers and hardly moving an inch, that was the reason. Directors had other problems. In silent films they used small ensembles, even a single violin out of picture to help create emotional and dramatic feelings in their actors and actresses. Sad music for tragedy; romantic music for romance; dramatic music for drama; gay music for happiness; sentimental music for sentiment. All this and the musicians had to be abandoned. Actors and actresses had to rely on themselves to get emotions across.

"Problems were legion. Technicians had to devise sound effects, like making a horse on the screen *sound* like a horse. They found a way, with empty halves of coconut shells and sand or oilcloth. They could make the shells sound like the clippety-clop of a horse. Lessen the speed, increase it, get the horse trotting, cantering, galloping, even just pawing the ground – coconut shells did it all. For jingling harness, they rattled a chain; a face slap was achieved by slapping two pieces of wood together; blood dripped effectively by tapping fingers on a hand.

"These are just a few examples of the ingenuity of early effects men. With those other pioneers, the sound men, the camera men, technical problems were gradually overcome."

With this new era of film-making, silent stars were the first to suffer. While they were fine in silent films, many of their voices did not register in sound. There followed a cascade of falling stars. The companies who decided to change over to talkies began importing established actors and actresses from the theatre, particularly from the New York stage. They could 'talk' and directors brought them to Hollywood – young stars like Charles Boyer, Edward G. Robinson, Ginger Rogers, Lucille Ball and many others. Once again there was a vast migration to the west, this time of actors and actresses who were sure they could make it in the talkies. Mass unemployment followed.

Bebe was one of the silent film stars to suffer. Ben Schulberg, head of Paramount production, was certain she wouldn't adapt to talkies. In future, he told her, they would be using stars from the theatre. Would they give her a voice test? she asked. The answer was – no, sorry, and Paramount dropped her. She had six months left of her contract with them and financially they honoured this. They did offer her a job as a writer, but Bebe refused. She was convinced that, given the chance, she could succeed in talkies. "But they were saying in Hollywood," Ben would recall, "Bebe Daniels is finished in films."

Bebe would laugh. "When my cousin Lee de Forest put sound on film, he nearly put me out of movies for good."

By now Bebe and Ben were seeing a great deal of each other. Ben did everything he could to help, but he was in no position to get her work. He, too, was faced with the problem of convincing directors that he could *talk*. Together they shared their uncertainties. Ben took Bebe out as much as possible and showed the Hollywood scene that he had no intention of forsaking her. But the gossip became too much for her. It was too sweet and sympathetic. Once again, keeping up the pretence that all was well when it wasn't and not letting anyone know what she intended to do, she let her house in Santa Monica to Norma Shearer and took an apartment in Los Angeles. Her mother went with her.

In their turn, stars who came to Hollywood from the theatre had problems. They faced a camera instead of a live audience. They were used to stage techniques. They had to learn the art form of the cinema. Learn it they did, with the help of directors. But Bebe knew the medium so well. It followed that she would find her place in talkies. She did this first in *Rio Rita*, forerunner of musical extravaganzas.

Stars and film-makers – they all set the scene for the coming of Hollywood's golden years. From its early beginnings, the speed and expansion of film-making was such that within twenty-five years Hollywood became the movie capital of the world. By 1930 silent films were becoming part of screen history.

17

Rio Rita

Bill le Baron who had been an executive at Paramount became head of a small film company called R.K.O. who were making 'quickies' (shorts). When he heard that Paramount had dropped Bebe he sent for her. He had faith in her work and knew her value as an actress.

"Of course you can talk," he told her – and he was certain she could make it in talkies. He couldn't offer her any immediate film part, but he signed her up under contract for a year, at a far less fee than she had been paid by Paramount. But Bebe was not concerned with fees. She was grateful that Bill le Baron believed in her sufficiently to offer her a contract at all. She returned to Los Angeles away from the gossips and waited.

At that time a musical, *Rio Rita*, was a hit in New York

and touring companies were playing it throughout America. Songs from the show were popular in America and Britain. While she was in her enforced retirement in Los Angeles, Bebe heard that R.K.O. was considering making a film of *Rio Rita*. She got a copy of the book, read it, and decided that if R.K.O. made a film version, she wanted to play Rita. But although she could sing — she had a natural singing voice — she realized this wasn't good enough.

Marion Davies was one of her close friends. "It was through Marion Davies that I had met the Italian opera singer, Signor Otto Morando," Bebe would recall, "so I went to see him. He agreed to give me lessons. When I tell you that Jeanette MacDonald studied with him — that's how good Otto Morando was as a teacher." She studied with him for four months, keeping quiet about what she was doing. People were curious; she was apparently doing nothing and the gossip continued that she was through in films. After the four months she was ready to see Bill le Baron about *Rio Rita*.

"Bill," she said, "I've read the book and I want to play Rita."

Bill le Baron shook his head. "Sorry Bebe — I'd love you to play it, but we want a singer."

"I can sing." No one in the film business seemed to know she could sing, even Bill le Baron.

He shook his head again. "We want an *opera*-type singer."

Bebe went on persisting that she could play the part. At last, impressed by her enthusiasm, Bill le Baron stopped saying "no". Certainly, he thought, she would make an ideal Rita with her dark hair and Spanish looks. He knew she wouldn't insist unless she meant it — or waste the studio time giving her a test unless she could sing. He gave her the score.

"I'll give you a voice test a week from today," he said. "Think you can do it?"

"Do it? You bet I'll do it! And Bill — thanks a million!" Recalling it all, Bebe would say, "I shall never forget the day. It was a Wednesday." With a week to study the score she went off in high spirits.

"But I immediately hit a snag. I would have to sing a high B-flat and I knew I couldn't. My range wasn't that high."

She was not the sort of person to panic, but at this

moment, "I felt very near to it." She immediately rang Otto Morando.

"Otto, I must see you. Can I come over right away?"

"Of course!" There was something in the urgency of her voice he could not ignore.

He listened patiently to her problem. "How long," she asked, "will it take me to reach a high B-flat?"

He shrugged – eloquently, spreading his hands.

"Maybe two or three weeks," he replied, "maybe never."

Something slipped in the pit of Bebe's stomach. She felt sick. "But Otto, I've got to be able to reach it in a week – by next Wednesday!"

He shrugged again.

"I know I can do it," she added. "I *will* do it – if you will help me."

Otto waded up and down the room for interminable seconds, his head bent, his chin cupped in one hand. He knew just what this meant for Bebe. She watched him anxiously, biting her bottom lip. Suddenly he turned and faced her.

"We start *now*!"

It was the moment when the threat of defeat turned into the promise of success. By the following Wednesday the high B-flat was perfect. So was the voice test for *Rio Rita*. A delighted Bill le Baron told an equally delighted Bebe, "You've got the part."

But, he explained to her, R.K.O. could not possibly afford to pay her anything like the high fees Paramount had paid her.

"That's okay with me," she said. "You believed in me when Paramount dropped me – remember? Let's not worry about money. Let's make the film a success."

She told R.K.O. she would be willing to take a small fee and a percentage of the gross earnings from the film. Naturally, neither she nor R.K.O. could guess whether it would be a success or not. But here was a small company and a team of people ready to work on a small fee basis and an unknown percentage. *Rio Rita was* a success. It grossed thousands of dollars. People in America, in Britain, and everywhere it was shown flocked to see the film. Critics raved about Bebe and her co-star John Boles – and it established her for all time as a talkie and singing star. Now she was famous and rich. It also established her as someone whose judgement in film-making could be relied upon. *Rio Rita* was also a tribute to Bill le Baron. In later years, she would say how grateful she was to him and to Otto Morando. "Without them I could never have made it, even though I believed in it . . . believing wasn't good enough."

Rio Rita took just twenty-one days to make. It was made in half black and white, half colour. Colour was now on the way and everyone went mad with reds in particular. *Everything* had to be colour, the brighter the better. We have seen the same thing in colour television – sober-voiced announcers wearing outlandish coloured ties and shirts.

With early technicolour films they opted for all shades of reds. So in the *Rio Rita* scene where Bebe was the bride, the wardrobe head wanted her to wear pink. She refused. The bridesmaids were wearing pink and she argued that a bride should be in white. Not because she was Bebe, but because she was convinced that a bride should be in white. The studio insisted pink. Bebe insisted white. She was on percentage so, although she didn't interfere in the production, this gave her the right to have some say. She won and wore white. The contrast effect of her white gown against the pink of the bridesmaids and other surrounding colours was, it was reported, "staggeringly beautiful".

"After that," Ben would say, "people sought her opinion and listened to her," adding, "No film of that magnitude could be made today in twenty-one days." Asked why, he replied, "There were no unions. People worked to *complete* a film in the shortest time possible and get on with the next."

The world première in Hollywood was attended by everybody who was anybody. Afterwards, Ben Schulberg of Paramount, who had dropped Bebe, stopped her and said, "Bebe, why didn't you tell me you could sing?"

She replied, "You didn't ask me."

That dialogue between her and Ben Schulberg was imprinted on her memory. Whenever she told it, she never varied it by a single word.

The romance of *Rio Rita* was echoed in real life. A month before shooting started, Bebe and Ben became engaged.

18

Winner Loses All

On the morning of 29 October 1929, Americans woke up to find the stock market had crashed overnight. A decade of post-war boom years and inflation was over. The economy had collapsed under the weight of inflation, engulfing hundreds of thousands of Americans in an avalanche of destitution, vast unemployment, hunger, bread lines, soup kitchens, bankruptcy. A stunned nation was floored like a boxer from an uppercut. The Great Depression set in. Fortunes were lost. Some men could not face bankruptcy, and the suicide rate was high.

Other men faced reality and began rebuilding the economy, but it would be some time before America could extricate herself. She was yet to go through the agonies of Prohibition and the gangster era.

Ben did not escape the stock market crash. He was no gambler. He had made a great deal of money in films and what he did with it, he thought was safe. He bought shares 'on margin', the nearest equivalent of buying everything you own on hire purchase. If something goes wrong and you can't pay you lose what you have. He didn't stop to think what would happen if the shares went down in value and he had to pay for them. Right now, he was making a handsome profit. When he told Bebe what he was doing, she didn't like the idea at all. She always said, "Pay for what you have outright. If you can't afford it, don't have it on the never-never." This was something her mother and Little Mother had taught her. From them she had learned to save and most of her money was invested in houses and land. So when Ben told her how he was playing the stock market, she was worried. One night, after he had coined in more profit, she said, "Darling it won't last. Why don't you put your money in a trust fund?"

He laughed outright. "A trust fund! Don't you realize? I'm making a profit without doing a thing!"

Bebe shook her head. "All right," she said, "if that's the way you want to do it . . . but Ben . . . "

"Yes, darling?"

"It won't last — it can't."

It didn't.

Suddenly, within hours, he needed fifteen thousand dollars to save being wiped out. He hadn't got that sort of money on hand. There was only one person he could possible ask. He picked up the phone and rang Howard Hughes.

Howard Hughes came at once to the phone.

"Howard . . . ", Ben explained briefly what had happened.

"How much do you need?" Howard Hughes asked.

"Fifteen thousand dollars."

"Get round here fast."

Ben drove fast to Hughes's house. Howard had already written out the cheque.

"It's a loan of course . . ." Ben began.

"Save the talk — you're welcome. Get it to your broker."

Another rush drive and the cheque was in the broker's hands. Ben left the office, shaking a little, sat in his car and thanked heaven for a friend like Howard Hughes. But it was too late. Wall Street had crashed irrevocably. Ben was wiped out. He had won Bebe, but he had lost all his money *and* the fifteen thousand dollars he had borrowed from Howard Hughes. He was back at the beginning. It was as if the clock had turned back to the time when he had no money and was struggling to succeed and survive.

And Bebe? The crash had hardly affected her. She owned four houses. One she had given to her mother; one to Little Mother; and she put Aunt Alma in another when her aunt and uncle hit a bad patch. But just as Ben had stood by her when everybody thought she was through, so now she stood by him. And Ben picked himself up, dusted himself down, and started all over again.

Film making survived and Hollywood prospered; in fact, people found an escape from the depression by going to cinemas. Ben made successful films and soon it was reported that he was one of the most sought after actors in Hollywood. And he made money. About that loan of fifteen thousand dollars from Howard Hughes?

"Forget it," said Howard.

Ben did not forget it. He repaid every cent.

19

Love and Marriage.... and Barbara

I did not know Bebe Daniels and Ben Lyon very well, but I always found their devotion to one another something very special and particularly rare in today's world.

Her Serene Highness Princess Grace de Monaco

Bebe and Ben were engaged for eighteen months before they married. There was no reason why they should not have married earlier, but both wanted to be sure that their marriage would be for all time.

"If we didn't know each other well enough after eighteen months to be as certain as we could be, then we guessed we never would," was Ben's summing up. And Bebe had the memory of her parents' broken marriage and the unhappiness of separation. Coincidentally, Ben's parents also separated, although their story had a happier ending and they were reunited. Ben blamed himself for their separation.

"I kept my mother in Hollywood too long," he said. "It was selfish of me, but at the time I thought I was doing the right thing."

Bebe and Ben's wedding on 30 June 1930 was reported as one of the "most beautiful in Hollywood that year." But even as Bebe walked up the aisle one Hollywood columnist had a pen poised to write, "it wouldn't last." In lasting nearly forty-one years, their marriage stilled that prediction.

Bebe had eight bridesmaids – Constance Talmadge, Lila Lee, Betty Compton, Mae Sunday – remembered today in the annals of those Hollywood years – Rita Kaufman, Diana Fitzmaurice, Mary Mosquini, and Adele Rogers St John. The dresses and hats were in tulle. Each two partners wore a pale and darker shade of yellow, pink, orchid and blue, and they carried matching coloured bouquets of roses. Louella Parsons was the Matron of Honour. Easter lilies and white blossom covered the altar. Like any bridegroom, Ben only had eyes for Bebe as she walked down the aisle towards him between banks of flowers lining the bridal path. One report afterwards which made them laugh described the banks of flowers lining the 'bridle' path. Bebe said, "I rode horses to school and in Westerns, but I didn't ride a horse down the aisle to my wedding!"

"She was breathtakingly beautiful," Ben would recall, "in sheer white against all that colour".

Columnists everywhere wrote up a description of her dress — "tight fitting with a long train of hand-woven ivory satin and Italian lace . . . a lace veil, yards long, she carried a bouquet of white orchids and lillies of the valley."

Bebe added: "I wore a little blue locket that belonged to Little Mother underneath my dress; Mary Pickford's lace handkerchief –that was 'something borrowed, something blue'. What I had on was 'something new'."

A hundred guests were at the wedding ceremony, four hundred at the reception. They spent their honeymoon in Santa Barbara, and they set up home in a beautiful Spanish-style home in Santa Monica, "with the Pacific Ocean as our front garden." Both were home-lovers; at the same time they started working in films again. In the years that followed an endless list of friends came to their home, among them the now legendary stars of Hollywood — Humphrey Bogart, Bing Crosby, Joan Crawford, Cary Grant, Irving Berlin, Gloria Swanson, Douglas Fairbanks and Mary Pickford, Norma Talmadge, Marion Davies, Clark Gable, Carole Lombard . . . Name them, they were there.

Among Bebe's well-remembered films was *42nd Street* made in 1933, in which she co-starred with Ginger Rogers, Ruby Keeler, Dick Powell and Warner Baxter. This was the era of the Busby ('Bus') Berkley extravaganzas, using hundreds of girls in fantastic choreography — from kaleidoscopic effects to aquabatics in a swimming pool. They had a catch-phrase for these films: "All Talking, All Singing, All Dancing." *42nd Street* was a showbiz story in which Bebe danced and sang 'You're Getting To Be A Habit With Me' as well as the title song.

This was the era in which successful songs were whistled by errand boys on bicycles. If they whistled your songs as they rode through streets delivering errands, you knew you had a success.

For some time Bing Crosby, "we loved the old groaner and his songs", was Bebe and Ben's neighbour in Santa Monica. Bebe played a scene with him – he was then a newcomer to films – in *Reaching For the Moon* in which she co-starred with Douglas Fairbanks, Snr.

Bing, Bebe and Ben often exchanged stories of Monseigneur Conneally, the priest who was famed in Hollywood for collecting from stars for the needy. Bing Crosby portrayed Monseigneur Conneally in the film based on his life, *Going My Way*.

"He was a great character," Ben would recall. "He would come to your home and say, 'You will give a hundred dollars for this charity or that charity' – and we gave it. One Christmas when he called on us he said to Bebe, 'This year Bebe you will give seventy-five turkeys.' What did she say? 'Yes Father' – and she gave seventy-five turkeys."

Each year, Monseigneur Conneally organized a Christmas charity show. One year, Bebe was working and she couldn't make it. She wrote to him, "I'm sorry I can't come Father, but I'll be there in spirit." Monseigneur Conneally replied, "Well, what seat does your spirit want to sit in – the twenty dollar one or the five dollar one?"

Was Hollywood a 'sin city'? In defending it against this description, Bebe said, "It did get that label at one time. Of course some people did wrong things. You find those sort of people in every city. But Hollywood film stars got so much publicity and so anything they did wrong was magnified and made public. As we all know, nothing is ever lost in the telling."

"I always remember," Ben added, "we were at a dance one night and they had one of those dances when the M.C. calls out different things he wants everyone to do. The drums rolled and he announced: 'Ladies and gentlemen, we are now going to have a happily married couples dance.' Everybody cheered and clapped and the music struck up. The M.C. said: 'First I want couples who have been married for a year to dance together.' Two or three couples got up, danced for a few minutes, the music stopped, they got a round of applause and went back to their tables. The M.C. said: 'Now I want couples who have been happily married for three years.' A few more couples got up. The same thing happened – they danced, they got their round of applause and sat down. Then he called for couples who'd been married five years. Even more couples got up. When he got to eight years, the floor was almost filled with dancers, including Bebe and me.

"It was the first time any of us had seen anything like this at a dance and the applause was getting deafening because we were all beginning to realize that despite the stories that went around about easy marriages in Hollywood and divorces, people were happily married there for *years*. I think the M.C. ended on about the fifteenth year – something like that. You see, good news isn't news. Anything sensational is, it seems . . . a pity, but there you are."

Bebe added, "You have only to think of Jack Benny and Mary Livingston; Phil Harris and Alice Faye; Joseph Cotten and Patricia Medina; Bob Hope and his wife. How long have they been married, Ben?"

"Goodness knows . . . years. Certainly as many years as we have – maybe more." And switching to another thought he said, "It *is* strange that people outside the business get the impression that Hollywood was night life, night clubs, dinner and supper parties, and swimming in magnificent garden pools. People didn't spend their days at race tracks and in swimming pools. That was the sort of idea that got around from photographs in movie magazines. We had to be up at six in the morning to be in make-up by seven o'clock and on the set by eight. We worked through the day, stopping to have a sandwich or two, and by the time we got home and had dinner it was time to go to bed; that would be about ten o'clock, so we could have a good night's sleep to be up again at six the next morning.

"You know something? When Bebe was with Paramount she worked for five years practically non-stop without a holiday – that was before we were married. She did take a holiday at last, but that'll give you some idea how film stars – not only Bebe – worked.

"Of course we enjoyed ourselves – it wasn't *all* work. We had some great times – and we played golf, tennis, squash, as well as swimming."

Film people played practical jokes on each other, and they

thought up quite the most fantastic things. For instance, when Hal Roach became the major stockholder in the Santa Anita racecourse and his birthday came round, Bebe hunted high and low for an old swathe-back truck horse. Swathe-back is a horse whose back sinks in the middle like a slight arch upside down. At last she found such a horse, bought it and had it delivered to Hal Roach's house, with strict instructions to the man that he was not to say who it was from and he was not to take it away again. The man duly arrived with the horse on Hal Roach's front lawn. He rang the door bell. Hal Roach came to the door and, as Bebe had instructed, the man said, "This horse is for you sir – the one you ordered."

Hal Roach gasped. "Me? Ordered that! There's some mistake – sorry."

The man replied: "No sir, there isn't. I've had strict instructions to deliver this horse to you," adding: "You are Mr Hal Roach?"

Hal Roach nodded: "Then this is your horse," the man said, handing him the reins. "Good luck sir with it on the race course." And off he went. Hal Roach was left standing holding the reins of a swathe-back horse which started chewing the grass on his front lawn. At first he was furious, but when Bebe admitted she had sent it as a joke, he enjoyed the episode as much as she did. What happened to the horse?

"We retired it," said Bebe, "put it out to pasture, poor old thing."

Ben also played jokes. He had an ostrich delivered to Douglas Fairbanks, Senr. "Doug sent me a goat, so I sent him an ostrich."

Another thing Bebe did at parties was to say before introducing a newcomer to a guest, "He's deaf." Then she and Ben and others would watch the result. The newcomer would either shout at the guest who wasn't deaf or try mouthing words. Puzzled, the guest would shrug, seek out Bebe and ask what was wrong with the other person. "I don't know," she would say, "what makes you think something's wrong with him?" She always told them in the end and they all had a good laugh.

And if she couldn't remember people's names, she got over

that by saying, if she had to introduce them, "You know each other, don't you?" – laugh gaily and leave two people together who didn't know each other from Adam.

When Bebe and Ben had free weekends, they sometimes spent these at the fabulous William Randolph Hearst's 'castle' ranch at San Simeon, described by them as "pure seventeenth century Italian. His art collection was priceless – Gainsborough and Rembrandt paintings, Gobelin tapestries. He collected furniture from all over the world. There were genuine Richelieu and Napoleon bedrooms. San Simeon was about two hundred and fifty thousand acres with thirteen miles of coastline. It had its own zoo, beautiful terraced gardens, everything you could want in the way of riding, swimming, tennis . . ."

Much has been written about the castle. In part the Orson Welles film *Citizen Kane* was supposedly based on San Simeon.

Basically Bebe and Ben were home builders and home lovers. This remained with them throughout their lives. They liked nothing more than friends coming to see them. Joan Crawford remembers those times in Hollywood:

> When I knew Bebe and Ben, I was so busy growing up and trying to learn my craft that I don't remember forming any opinions of them except to love them dearly, because they were so kind to me. They were very much established stars when I arrived in Hollywood, but they were always real and warm friends, and always invited me to their beach home in Santa Monica on Sundays for a swim and beautiful lunch. We have kept in touch through the years, which proves a firm and loyal friendship.

Did they argue? Bebe said, "We have a pact. When one of us wants to argue, the other shuts up. Nobody can argue with themselves."

Barbara was born on 9 September 1931.

Bebe was filming up to three months before Barbara was born and she did not want the news to get out. She still had to finish the film, so she went on working until her commitment was completed. But she did go round buying baby clothes. Louella Parsons was the first to suspect and one day she rang Bebe.

"I want you to tell me truthfully," she asked her, "are you going to have a baby?"

Louella Parsons was often feared by people in Hollywood because of what she might write about them, but Bebe and Ben always said that if you told Louella the truth and asked her not to publish something, she wouldn't do so. If you evaded her or told a deliberate lie and she found out — "God help you."

Without hesitation Bebe said, "Yes Louella, I'm going to have a baby, but I want to finish the film I'm doing and it wouldn't do to let the news out at the moment."

"Well, that's great news," said Louella. "I won't say a word until you tell me I may."

As soon as Bebe was ready for the story to break, she rang Louella Parsons. Louella was first with the news.

The birth was a particularly difficult one and afterwards Bebe had to rest for about four months. But she wasn't the sort of person who could sit around with her feet up and do nothing. As soon as she was able she got friends together and they played quite a lot of bridge. This was fine at first because they came to her house, but now they said, "You must come to us . . . get out of the house."

Bebe wouldn't go out for an afternoon's bridge and leave Barbara to a nursemaid. She knew she would have to do this when she went back to work, but for the moment, "I wanted my baby with me." So she took Barbara with her in a carry cot, and with the baby alongside her, played bridge. When Barbara grew up, she became an avid card player. She does, in fact, play bridge, canasta, and most card games expertly. Barbara's comment, "Can you wonder, when mother weaned me on cards?"

Barbara was four months old when Bebe went back to the theatre. She starred in *The Last of Mrs Cheyney* which had successful runs in San Francisco and Los Angeles; then she returned to films.

Ben was always a keen photographer. In their Santa Monica home, Bebe and Ben had a projection room which was like a small cinema. Here they ran 'rushes' of their films so that they could be self-critical of their work; or they ran films to friends for an evening's entertainment, as well as home movies.

From the time Barbara was born, Ben took snaps and later movies of her, including the conventional pictures of her lying naked on her stomach on a rug. In later years, when she was growing up and going out with her first boyfriends, if she didn't toe the line — and Bebe and Ben were very strict about spoiling her in any way — he would simply have to say to her, "If you don't behave, I'll show George or Jim ..." or whatever her latest boyfriend's name was ... "that picture of you as a baby naked on the rug".

"Daddy," she would say, "you wouldn't dare!"

Barbara could never find out where her father hid those pictures, "but he could produce them at the drop of a hat!"

Asked about her theory on bringing up Barbara, Bebe replied, "I have never had any special theory about bringing up my daughter, believing that if I raised her as my mother raised me, I would be doing a pretty good job. So from the time Barbara was a tot, I treated her as my best friend and confidant. In our family circle, we speak to each other on the same level — even when it comes to criticism."

20

American Maid

Things had gone wrong in the past. They might go wrong in the future. This was how Bebe and Ben figured. They were on top in show business. But who could tell what might happen? So, with their friends Pauline and Skeets Gallagher — they played with Skeets Gallagher in the stage comedy *Hollywood Holiday* — they invested in a shop in Westwood featuring ladies' sportswear and calling it 'American Maid'. It proved so successful that they opened more shops, one of them next to the 'Brown Derby', a famous restaurant. Others were opened in Palm Springs and on Catalina Island. Business was so good that they opened a factory, designing and manufacturing their own sportswear to cut out the middle man. From the factory they sold not only in their own shops, but to leading stores like Saks Fifth Avenue, Neiman-Marcus in Dallas, Texas, Bon Marché in San Francisco — stores in *i/*

America equivalent to Harrods, Selfridges, Harvey Nichols, Dickens & Jones in England.

Altogether, eighty-five people were employed in the factory. Two years later, they lost their cutter. A cutter is important to any dress factory and they had to apply to the appropriate union for another cutter. A man was sent with highest references and he was first-class. Some weeks later samples of new sportswear designs were taken out on the road throughout the States by the salesmen. Orders for hundreds of dozens of the various models were received. These were cut, made up and sent out. Within two weeks all were returned as 'unacceptable', due to faults like shoulders being lopsided, waistlines being too high. Hems were also lopsided and sleeves uneven in length. It transpired that somehow a rival concern had been able to send in the new cutter and he was in a position to sabotage the business. He was fired, but it was too late. Bebe realized she was not equipped to complete in such a cut-throat business and the factory was closed with a loss of forty-seven thousand dollars. Added to this, other personal friends in the film industry had invested in the factory. Bebe paid them back the full amount they had invested. She never wanted a friend to say they had lost money with her.

After this, Ben said, "No more investments."

But he had an inventive mind. Because of his experience as a flier, he thought up car seat belts long before anyone else. He took the idea to motoring organizations but nothing happened.

When he and Bebe first came to England he noticed women often pushing linen, presumably to a laundry, in prams or pushchairs. America had already opened up launderettes and he thought it would be wonderful to bring these to Britain. He went into it thoroughly and put up the idea to companies who might be interested in opening launderettes. People who might have been interested shook their heads. "No," they said, "it would never catch on in Britain."

After a time they realized that whenever they tried to step outside their life in show business, things would not go right. But fate plays strange tricks on people. Hal Roach offered them shares in the newly proposed Santa Anita rececourse, as famous in California as Epsom is in England. Bebe was excited by this prospect; but Ben said a firm, "No!" The racecourse made a fortune for the shareholders.

On occasions, Bebe had a flutter on horse racing. She always backed the jockeys, not the horses, and invariably she won. Ben, on the other hand, was the unluckiest racing gambler ever. The year Red Alligator won the Grand National, Bebe and I backed it, simply because we liked the name. Ben refused to put a bet on. Then about five minutes before the race started – we were going to watch it on television – he changed his mind. He rang a bookmaker and put five shillings each way on a horse he picked. It fell at the first fence.

Bebe's most disastrous racing story began the day she had lunch with some girlfriends. The next day was the St Leger. Her girlfriends wanted to back a horse, but they didn't know a bookmaker. Bebe knew two bookmakers by the names of Mossy Brown and Mossy Green, so the girls pooled their money, gave it to her, and she put it on. The horse won at a high price – and Mossy Brown and Mossy Green vanished! Bebe didn't say a word. She paid out. Her friends never knew that their bet cost her about £75.

It wasn't always like that; but, as a reporter said in 1938 in the *Star*, London's third evening paper then in circulation, "They have a disarming way of telling stories against themselves."

21

Enter Al Capone

The theatre and films have always mirrored the times. Wars have produced war plays and films. Peace and prosperity have produced lavish musicals.

When the American government passed the Prohibition Law in June 1920, which was not repealed until 1933, it sparked off more than a decade of violence and crime hitherto unknown in the States. A new breed of criminal mushroomed in parts of America – the gangster. In life and death duels, guns blazed as rival gangs mowed each other down. Gambling and protection rackets sprang up. Plots were hatched in smoke-laden gaming rooms. The hotbed of their world was Chicago. As gangsters fought among themselves, federal agents fought the gangsters. It all got on the screen.

Movie gangsters like Humphrey Bogart, James Cagney and Edward G. Robinson played tough-guy roles and 'died' over and over again in films. Bebe and Ben had acted with them, although not in gangster films. Then a real gangster came briefly and unexpectedly into their lives.

They had gone to Chicago to appear in a play. During its run, Bebe's jewellery was stolen from her hotel room. The theft was reported in the press and suddenly her jewellery was returned intact. The man who got it back for her was Al Capone. When he read about the theft he gave orders to the underworld that the jewellery was to be found and returned to her. Unknown to Bebe, Capone was a great admirer of hers, but she never actually met him. He did invite Bebe and Ben to his apartment, but they were leaving Chicago almost immediately and were unable to accept. Later they learnt that Capone's apartment was built of steel, with sliding steel doors, and henchmen guarded the apartment with machine guns.

In March 1932 another sinister event burst upon the American people – kidnapping. Posters and massive press reports announced the kidnapping of Charles A. Lindbergh, Jnr., son of Col. Charles A. Lindbergh, the world-famous pioneer transatlantic aviator, fêted by his country as a hero. The posters read, with photographs of the twenty-month-old baby, "This child was kidnapped from his home in Hopewell, N.J. between eight and ten p.m. on Tuesday March 1 1932." Agonising weeks followed for Charles Lindbergh and his wife before and after their baby son's body was found near their home. Finally the kidnapper, Bruno Hauptmann, was caught and brought to trial early in 1935.

Child kidnapping did not end with the Lindbergh tragedy. In time it would reach Hollywood.

22

And So To Britain

In 1933 Bebe and Ben, with Sally Eilers, were invited to
Britain to tour theatres. Their studios in Hollywood released
them to do the tour.

Bebe and Ben with Barbara, now two-and-a-half years old,
a nursemaid, a secretary, and a mountain of luggage, arrived
in Britain. To be more precise they arrived from Plymouth at
the Great Western Railway terminus in London. Awaiting
their arrival was an army of pressmen and photographers. As
Ben put it: "We were that strange breed from Hollywood.
People had seen us on the screen, now here we were in the
flesh. We were amazed and pleased to find so many people
had come along to say 'hullo'. We didn't expect it; we
thought we'd just arrive and go to our hotel. But we got a real
British welcome — something we've talked about many times.
We guess we kind of walked out of the screen on to that
British railway platform . . ."

Ben is a born organizer. While photographers clicked away
and pressmen talked, five taxis were called to take him and
Bebe, Barbara, the nursemaid, the secretary and the luggage
to their hotel. Bebe and Ben would ride in the first taxi, the
nursemaid, Barbara and the secretary in the second, and the
luggage in the other three. Ben organized it all. At last the
procession was ready to move off.

"Where to, guv?" asked the taxi driver through the
communicating window. As Bebe and Ben waved to the
crowd gathered round their cab, Ben said: "Great Western
Hotel." The taxi driver scratched his head and said slowly,
"You're at the Great Western Hotel." Ben had no idea that
hotels were a part of railway stations. There was nothing for
it but to get out of the station. With all the organizing he had
been doing, getting everyone and the luggage settled in the
taxis, Ben couldn't get them all out again. He thought fast.
"Drive round the block," he told the driver. So the retinue
left the station, drove round and round the streets until they
were sure the press and public had gone; then they returned

to the Great Western Hotel, where they disembarked. It is not recorded what the other four taxi drivers thought of American idiosyncracies as they followed the first cab – and finally back to the station.

Later, the family moved to the Dorchester in Park Lane, a little less noisy than steam trains pulling out almost from under their bedroom windows.

Bebe and Ben travelled round the provinces making personal appearances, and wherever they went audiences gave them a tremendous welcome. The British liked them – and they thought the British were "great – just great!"

During their stay in Britain, they were invited with Sally Eilers to the Duke and Duchess of Sutherland's home. When Ben told one of his favourite stories of that occasion, he did so with appropriate actions. He often enacted stories in this way, making them doubly entertaining for appreciative guests. Of this story, he seated three guests on the sofa in the living room and said, "Now you are Bebe, Sally and myself." Hunching his shoulders, his arms widespread, he emulated a butler carrying a large silver tray. "I must tell you," he said, "this was the first time we'd seen an English butler in full dress livery. He was a magnificent figure." At the sofa, he bowed majestically to the three occupants, offering them the imaginary tray. "What do you think was on it?" he asked. All three shook their heads. "Three strips of chewing gum, one for each of us! The British really thought all Americans chewed gum! Our expressions must have given us away as we said, 'No, thank you.' The Duke came over, took a piece himself and said, 'I love it,' and we realized he was kidding us. Anyway, we all had a good laugh."

With so much to talk about, it never surprised me that guests who came at 5.30 p.m. for an hour and a cocktail were still there and reluctant to leave at 8.30 p.m.!

On another occasion in London, a ball at Grosvenor House was attended by the Prince of Wales. After formal present-ations, it was one of Bebe's more treasured memories that the Prince asked her to dance with him.

Too soon, the studios in Hollywood recalled Bebe, Ben and Sally to make more pictures. Bebe co-starred with John Barrymore in *Counsellor at Law*, Ben with Claudette Colbert

in *I Cover The Waterfront*. This was followed by a theatre
tour of the comedy *Hollywood Holiday* with Skeets Gallagher.

During the run of this play the threat of kidnapping hit
them. They heard through the police that there was a threat
to kidnap Barbara. This was frightening news after the
Lindbergh case.

"We immediately arranged for an armed guard for Barbara," said Ben, "an ex-heavyweight prize fighter to live in
the house. Bebe's mother and Little Mother also lived in the
house, so Barbara was well taken care of until we could get
home and nothing more happened."

Then threats of kidnapping started again early in 1935.
The scare really hit Hollywood. Harold Lloyd's children were
guarded day and night, so were the children of Norma
Shearer, Mary Pickford, Darryl Zanuck. They were all
threatened and another threat came to kidnap Barbara,
demanding ten thousand dollars ransom. Buron Fipps, the
Attorney-General, and a friend of Bebe and Ben's, advised
them to take Barbara to Europe until the situation quietened
down. So they returned to Britain.

For a time they stayed at the Dorchester again and toured
the country working in theatres, including the London
Palladium, associated for so many years with one of the
legendary names of the theatre, impresario Val Parnell. Bebe
and Ben's appearances at the London Palladium were the
beginning of a close friendship between them and Val Parnell
and his wife Helen.

As it seemed they would be based on London for some
time, they took a house in Buckingham Gate, near Buckingham Palace. They admired the King and Queen; they were
proud to be near the Palace; and they were now feeling very
much a part of Britain, so they hung out a Union Jack from
the first-floor window. The next day the doorbell rang. Their
secretary answered the door and returned to the living-room
to tell them, "it's the police."

"Police!" Ben exploded. "Bebe, what have you been
doing?"

"Nothing," she replied.

"Are you sure?"

"Positive." She laughed. "What have *you* been doing?"

Ben thought quickly. Nobody could be in an accident. Barbara and the nursemaid were in the house. There was no kidnap scare in Britain. As far as he could remember he hadn't driven on the wrong side of the road. Well, he'd soon get to the bottom of it. "Ask him in," he told the secretary.

The policeman came into the room respectfully carrying his helmet.

"Come on in, officer," said Ben. "What's the trouble?"

"Well, no trouble sir — but is everything all right?"

Ben sighed with relief. This was something! A British police officer calling round to ask if everything was all right. "Everything's fine," he said, "Isn't it Bebe?"

"Fine . . . nothing's wrong at all."

They were mystified but pleased to have all this attention.

"That's all right then," said the policeman, "but we wondered, seeing that you're Bebe Daniels and Ben Lyon . . ."

Again thoughts of kidnapping rushed through Ben's mind. Not here in Britain, surely?

The policeman went on, "Is that your Union Jack hanging outside the window?"

"Why, yes," said Bebe. "Shouldn't it be there?"

"Oh yes, it's all right for it to be there but . . ." the policeman smiled, "you've hung it upside down and that's a distress signal."

Bebe and Ben were still in England on 2 November 1936, the *official* Opening Day of the B.B.C. Television Service.

Cecil Madden, a pioneer producer/programme organizer and later a controller of B.B.C. Television, was responsible for creating and producing many of those early programmes. On the second day of the Official Opening in his 'Starlight' programme at 3.45 p.m., Bebe and Ben were the stars. They were the first Americans to appear on the B.B.C. Television Service, headlined: *The First Television Service in the World.*

Cecil Madden recalls:

"Here is the actual billing on the afternoon of the second day of the first Television Service in London, and consequently in the world, from the B.B.C.'s Alexandra Palace Studios:

And So To Britain

3.45 p.m. Tuesday, November 3rd 1936
Starlight
BEBE DANIELS AND BEN LYON
The Hollywood Film Stars

In this series stars in every walk of life will appear. Bebe Daniels and Ben Lyon are names well known to Cinemagoers. One of Bebe Daniels' successes was in *Rio Rita* and in this act she may sing one or two numbers from it. Ben Lyon her husband has been in many outstanding film productions such as *Hell's Angels* and *I Cover the Waterfront*.

"Keen to be the first front-rank stars to appear on the new medium, the reason they first appeared in an afternoon transmission – and one must remember that at that time there were only 300 TV sets in homes in the London area – was because they were that week starring at the local Wood Green Empire in variety otherwise they would have been in the evening programme.

"Sophie Tucker had told me that she wanted to be the first American top star to appear on the very first television service in the world but in the event she was beaten to it by Bebe and Ben, and the American Cabaret comedian Lou Holtz on December 5th."

In 1937 they toured South Africa, taking Barbara with them. Barbara was now six years old. This was to prove one of the most exciting events in a six year old's life. For Bebe and Ben their voyage in the *Stirling Castle*, which took seventeen days in 1937 to reach Cape Town, was memorable; it heralded the tremendous reception they would have as they toured South Africa giving personal theatre performances in Cape Town, Pietermaritzburg, Johannesburg, Durban, Pretoria, and Port Elizabeth.

"When I tell you," Ben would recall, "that it is a thousand miles from Cape Town to Johannesburg and another thousand from Johannesburg to Durban, you can imagine the distances we travelled. We really saw South Africa. We also went to Kimberley the famous diamond-mining town in the Cape Province. Nobody gave us any diamonds, but we met two wonderful people, Doris and James Jones. All through the years we have kept in touch with Doris and James."

The theatre tour was arranged by Jack MacKenzie of African Consolidated Theatres.

"We also went into native villages," said Bebe. "I remember one tribal chief had eleven wives! In another village the tribesmen put on one of their ceremonial dances. These dances are something to watch!"

Wherever they went, crowds gathered to greet them. Johannesburg declared a public holiday when they arrived there. Paul Irwin of *The Rand Daily Mail*, Johannesburg, wrote this account of that day after Bebe died in 1971, under the headline:

WHEN BEBE RODE UP ELOFF STREET

Do you remember the afternoon when Bebe Daniels and her husband, Ben Lyon, came riding up Eloff Street — the first Hollywood big-name film stars to visit Johannesburg?

If you do remember, then it's a fair bet that you are among the over 40s. And if you will not confess to that, you must have been knee high to a couple of tickeys as Bebe and Ben passed by.

It was on September 25, 1937, that the husband-wife acting team arrived in our town by train from the Cape. Don't tell me I'm wrong. I looked it up in the yellowing files of this family newspaper.

Yes, looked it up yesterday when over the teleprinter came a Sapa-Associated Press message to say that dear, delightful Bebe Daniels had died a few hours earlier at her London home.

On the Monday after the stars' arrival, accompanied by Billy Costello, the original Sailorman for the old "Popeye" cartoons, and screen personalities Zelma O'Neal and Len Young, the Rand Daily Mail really spread itself.

The story was told of Bebe and Ben driving along Eloff Street under clouds of paper hurled by thousands of cheering fans.

Not only that, the train bringing them from Cape Town was more than 30 minutes late. as if that was something unusual for South African trains. Perhaps it was in 1937.

Reason for the delay: crowds at every station along the line clamoured to see Bebe and her husband.

Bebe was the showpiece, and why not? Here she was in the flesh: the glamourous singing star of Rio Rita, one of the earliest of the musicals when talkies nudged out silent films for keeps.

Over the telephone yesterday, Mr. A.H. ("Jim") Stodel, executive director of South African Consolidated Theatres, recalled the Johannesburg welcome for Bebe and Ben.

"It was the city's first Lindbergh-style welcome," he said. "Home after flying the Atlantic solo, Lindbergh rode through New York under a snowstorm of ticker-tape and pages torn from telephone books.

Johannesburg was a bit short on ticker-tape and telephone books. However, the film fans lined Eloff Street and showered Bebe, Ben and the rest of them, with everything from newsprint to old exercise books filched off the kids.

"We couldn't have wished for anything better to boost publicity for the vaudeville show put on by the visiting Americans at the Empire Theatre. And boy, did the customers set the box-office working overtime? I'll say they did."

There you have it. A memory of old, far-off, happy days. And if the Near-40s and Over-40s aren't humming the theme song from Rio Rita as they read this column piece, you can knock me down with a bit of ticker-tape.

Finally they returned to Britain: more theatre shows; more television; more radio – not only with the B.B.C. but, to quote Ben, "over the airwaves of Radio Luxemburg and Normandy, the then commercial broadcasting systems which people could hear in Britain if they tuned in to those stations. There was no commercial broadcasting in Britain. Oh yes, I forgot to mention – Paris also had its broadcasting system, beaming these sort of programmes to Britain. The way it worked was by making recordings in this country arranged by the J. Walter Thompson advertising agents and flying them out to the commercial stations on the Continent. It was through these broadcasts that we worked with people like Tommy Handley, Jack Hylton and other British stars."

1937 was an eventful year. Bebe and Ben had always wanted a son; besides, they did not want Barbara to be brought up as an only child. In that year Richard completed the family.

So into 1938 and 1939 – busy years, making films in Britain as well as continuing radio, television and theatre shows.

War Onwards...

23

War...... And Hi Gang!'

Harry Alan Towers wrote a book on the history of the B.B.C. Bebe
and Ben weren't even mentioned in that book — not any of their
programmes or what they did during the war. If anyone deserved
mention — Bebe and Ben did. How anyone could ever write a book
about the B.B.C. and not mention them is beyond me.

At the same time they were never honoured by Britain for
choosing to stay with the British rather than return to the safety of
America when war broke out. If Ben had been knighted and Bebe
had become Lady Lyon — that would have been justice. I was all for
some recognition — so was Anna. But it never happened.

Herbert Wilcox

With the rumblings of war in the uneasy summer of 1939,
Bebe and Ben sent Barbara and Richard back to California
with Bebe's mother. The rumblings continued as Adolf
Hitler's war machine rolled across Europe.

At 11 a.m. on Sunday, 3 September 1939, Neville
Chamberlain made his historic broadcast that Britain and
France were at war with Germany. Bebe and Ben were in
Blackpool appearing in one of Val Parnell's shows. Val
Parnell was also in Blackpool. He rushed over to their hotel.
Sadly he said to them, "Well, this is it. What are you going to
do?"

They had already made their decision. "We're staying,"
they said.

In later years, asked why they decided to stay, Bebe
replied, "The British had been so wonderful to us, we
couldn't run out on them when they were in trouble."

A few days later the American Government advised them,
as they did all Americans in Britain, to go home. If they
stayed their Government could not guarantee their safety.
Bebe and Ben had already made their decision to stay. They
found the London house they wanted, 18 Southwick Street,
in the Paddington area, a tall, thin, typical London house,
with a basement, ground floor and four floors above; and
with steps leading up to the front door. The door was

important. Bebe and Ben had it painted blue, so it became known as "the house with the blue door". It was a happy house. It was a busy house. "People were in and out like Paddington Station," Ben would say. Here 'Hi Gang!' and 'Life With The Lyons' were conceived. The house was 'home' to many American and British servicemen during the war.

Louella Parsons once said, "All you have to do when you arrive in London is to say to the taxi driver — Take me to Bebe and Ben's home, and he will take you right there."

They toured theatres, factories, forces camps, all over Britain, and entertained a new kind of army which sprang up everywhere called the Home Guard. The Home Guard is portrayed on radio and television today in 'Dad's Army', featuring Arthur Lowe as the earnest Captain Mainwaring, determined to protect King and Country with his 'company', portrayed by John Le Mesurier, Clive Dunn, John Laurie, James Beck as Private Walker the wide boy who can get anything on the black market, Arnold Ridley and Ian Lavender. With all the humour attached to 'Dad's Army' there is more than a grain of truth.

On 20 June 1942, a special concert was given at Buckingham Palace in the presence of Their Majesties King George VI and Queen Elizabeth, other members of the Royal Family and their friends. The concert was in support of the Buckingham Palace Home Guard. This was the programme:

Artists

ARTHUR ASKEY

SIDNEY BURCHALL

BENNETT AND WILLIAMS

COL-LING-SOO
Accompanist, HILDA BERTRAM

ESTHER COLEMAN
Accompanist, JIMMY BARRY

BEBE DANIELS AND BEN LYON
Accompanist, MATT HEFT

PAT GUEST

LESLIE HENSON—STANLEY HOLLOWAY
Accompanist, Mrs. G. Dodd

NOSMO KING AND HUBERT

HARRY KORRIS (Mr. Lovejoy)
ROBBIE VINCENT (Enoch)
CECIL FREDERICK (Mr. Ramsbottom)

JESSIE MATTHEWS
Accompanist, Bob Busby

DONALD PEERS

ANNE SHELTON
Accompanist, Stanley Black

MANNING SHERWIN—EILEEN HUNTER

JACK TRAIN

ELSIE AND DORIS WATERS

WESTERN BROTHERS (Kenneth and George)

VAL GUEST	JIMMY BARRY
Compere	*Accompanist*

STRING BAND OF H.M. GRENADIER GUARDS
Lieut. F. J. Harris, *Director of Music*

"Afterwards," said Ben, "when I was washing my hands, I looked longingly at the towel with the royal crest on it. I would have loved to have taken it as a souvenir. But if it had been discovered, can you imagine the headline: 'Ben Lyon steals towel from Buckingham Palace'!" Years later, Ben was a guest on radio's 'Sounds Familiar' programme. Max Jaffa another guest, told a story of appearing with other artists before Their Majesties and the Royal Family at Buckingham Palace. Afterwards, tea was arranged for the artists in an ante-room. They waited quite a long time; then a footman appeared and apologized – the kettle had broken down. Without hesitation and to the accompaniment of laughter from the audience, Ben came in with, "If they will send me a towel, I'll send them a kettle."

129

But back to the war.

Along with the fighting services, the B.B.C. became the Fourth Arm. If you couldn't fight the Nazis with weapons, you fought them with words and humour – a trait for which the British are renowned in times of crisis. Look at some of our cartoonists' work: Giles, Cummings, Osbert Lancaster, and so many others. During the war the *Daily Express* cartoonist, Strube, depicted the little man for ever struggling on through the blitz and other crises. After the war he did a picture in colour of his little man wearing a somewhat battered bowler hat and crumpled suit, his spectacles not quite straight, standing outside the stage door of a theatre. He is holding an enormous bouquet woven into a circle. Across the middle is the single word 'Bebe'. The stage doorkeeper is peering at him and saying, "I tell you she's gorn to America." To this, Strube's little man is replying, "Then I'll wait until she comes back." The picture always hung in Bebe and Ben's home, one of their treasured possessions.

Again, though, this is running ahead of time. It was still war. One day Ben said to Bebe, "Look, darling, we're going all over the country trying to entertain as many people as we can. Why don't we put up an idea to the B.B.C. for a programme that will reach many more people at the same time?" So the idea of 'Hi Gang!' was born. They asked Vic Oliver if he would join them. Without hesitation he agreed. He and Bebe wrote a pilot script. They took the idea to Pat Hillyard, Head of B.B.C. Light Entertainment. It was accepted and 'Hi Gang!' went on the air. Many people will remember the opening music played by Jay Wilbur and his Orchestra, 'I'm Just Wild About Harry', Ben's cheery introduction, 'Hi Gang!' – and the audience replying, 'Hi Ben!' It was a gay, new type of radio show in Britain, with a high standard of comedy, fast-moving action, gags and wisecracks galore. The British caught on fast to wisecracking among themselves. The programme also made fun of Hitler and 'Lord Haw-Haw' (William Joyce the traitor) whose sinister rhetoric of wartime propaganda was heard in Britain. He came on the air announcing, 'This is Germany calling' – pronouncing Germany like 'Jarmany'.

As well as being sinister it was a cajoling voice, telling the British it was no use their going on, and giving deceptive statistics of losses on land, sea and in the air. Unlike the Germans and occupied countries whose people were forbidden to listen to British radio, there was no such restriction in Britain to listening to Germany. So we listened to Lord Haw-Haw and laughed at him. Bebe and Ben did a show called *Haw-Haw* at London's Holborn Empire until it was bombed, fortunately at night after the theatre was closed. However, they continued their fun and laughter in 'Hi Gang!' – one of the B.B.C. shows which never left London.

When bombing started in 1940, certain B.B.C. programmes were moved out of London to Evesham, Bangor, and Bristol. They all added up to a vast network of studios spread over the country. If one studio got bombed out, another could take over. The main thing – the B.B.C. must never go off the air. It never did.

As well as having their own radio shows, appearing in theatres or entertaining the forces, stars like Jack Buchanan, Sarah Churchill, Noel Coward, Florence Desmond, Geraldo, Carroll Gibbons, John Gielgud, Robertson Hare, Stanley Holloway, Michael Redgrave, Jack Warner, and many others, appeared as guests in 'Hi Gang!' The programme started broadcasting from studios in Maida Vale. Bombed out from there, it moved to St George's Hall near Broadcasting House, and finally ended up in the Paris Cinema in Lower Regent Street, taken over by the B.B.C. as a wartime underground studio. The Paris is still one of its studios.

It is history that when Adolf Hitler ranted that he would "wring the British neck like a chicken", and Winston Churchill retorted. "Some chicken . . . some neck!", the whole nation stuck out its neck and invited Hitler to wring it. Showbiz people fought their brand of warfare with him, cutting him down to size by making people laugh at him. 'Hi Gang!' was one of the 'cutting Hitler down to size' radio programmes. After the war, Bebe and Ben learned that their names were high on the Führer's list for extermination if the Nazis had ever conquered Britain. 'Hi Gang!' ran for two-and-a-half years. Not only was it heard in Britain and Commonwealth countries, but resistance groups and others in

German-occupied Europe heard it. In peril of their lives, these people tuned in to B.B.C. radio programmes.

Bebe introduced a new song every week into the show. One of these, 'The White Cliffs of Dover', has often been sung by Vera Lynn as a popular wartime song. Music and songs, like the theatre and films, reflect the times in which we live and an abundance of songs came out of the war. Mikhail Glinka once wrote, "A nation creates music — the composer only arranges it."

Dame Anna Neagle, writing in The Silent Picture, Summer/Autumn 1971, recalled her memories of 'Hi Gang!':

> I was privileged to read the lesson at the funeral service of Bebe at the Church of Edward the Confessor. The Church was filled to overflowing by her friends and admirers and, as I waited to go to the lectern, my mind went back to memories of her. One picture came vividly to mind: it was during the war years — 1941 to be precise. Cuddled up in the corner of an enormous settee in the drawing room of her home, Bebe, virtually dictating her ideas for one of the 'Hi Gang' radio' shows. Ben was, as always, by her side. Vic Oliver and Tom Ronald, the producer, were there. Bebe's mind was crystal clear, as she heard, and visualized, every idea that she, or the others, put forward. How little the invaluable work Bebe and Ben did throughout the war was recognized is unfortunate, but the millions of listeners who were lifted out of the gloom was ample reward for two wonderful people — and artists — who, as American citizens could have justifiably been in Hollywood earning big money and eating regularly at Romanoffs or Chasens, instead of war-time rations in England.
>
> The 'Hi Gang' shows were broadcast from the Paris Cinema in Lower Regent Street and I recall the alert went in the middle of the performance. We all hurried from the stage to the stairs and sat waiting for the 'All Clear'. The noise of enemy planes and gunfire was so heavy — and close — someone had forgotten to close the roof! We all dashed down to the packed basement and how we laughed — none louder than Bebe.

And Herbert Wilcox recalls:

One thing I remember during the war Anna and I were having supper with Bebe and Ben at 18 Southwick Street. We had curried eggs. If you think there's nothing unusual in that — our ration per person was one fresh egg a month. Bebe and Ben had a friend in the country who sent them a few fresh eggs. It was typical — they shared them with us and Vic Oliver . . . he was there too. We had gone to their house to talk about a 'Hi Gang!' programme with Bebe and Ben and

Vic. Bebe — an absolute dynamo — was full of ideas for the programme all the time . . . but I was only interested in those curried eggs and rice!

On another occasion Anna and I had to miss a 'Hi Gang!' show because suddenly at the last minute we were asked to go to Canada by Air Marshal Bishop. When 'Hi Gang!' went on the air someone announced the reason: "We are sorry our friends Anna Neagle and Herbert Wilcox can't be with us — they have just left on their way to Canada."

This was a fatal thing to say. When we got to Glasgow to board a ship, security people were there to meet us. Instead of going to the Caledonian Hotel where we were booked in, we were taken to another hotel we had never heard of. Security people guarded us everywhere. Then we were taken on a train a long way away — and finally after roundabout journeys still securely guarded, we were put on a ship *The Batory* — a Polish ship. It was all very cloak and dagger. And all because of this slip of the tongue by an announcer saying we were going to Canada. The Germans weren't after us, but they could have had us followed and that would have given them vital information of ship movements. That's how strict security was — and that's how we came to miss one 'Hi Gang!' show.

Daphne Frizell remembers:

When I was in my teens I used to go to rehearsals of 'Hi Gang!' with my mother and sisters. It was always exciting because we were brought up in show business — the Tin Pan Alley side of the business. My father, Charles Lucas, was with the music publishers, Francis, Day and Hunter — he used to work on arrangements, I remember, for Bebe's songs. I didn't see Bebe and Ben again for many years; then I met them when they lived in Dolphin Square. To me they hadn't changed over the years. They were just the same in themselves. Bebe and I sang songs from those 'Hi Gang!' days — and we sang 'You're Getting To Be A Habit With Me' from *Forty-second Street*. We sang quietly and to ourselves, but it was fun remembering. My admiration for them was great — their marriage and their devotion for one another. I'm sure I'm not alone in saying — we miss them.

During weekend breaks, Bebe and Ben sometimes spent a couple of days with Val and Helen Parnell in their home at Princes Risborough, when they could all get there. One weekend, with Helen they picked mushrooms in the fields to take back to people in London. A lone Nazi fighter, returning from a raid, saw them. He dived and tried to strafe them with machine-gun fire. They flung themselves into a ditch, spilling the mushrooms. They came out of the ditch unharmed, "but we were furious," said Ben. "We lost all our mushrooms and went back to London empty-handed."

This outlook is borne out by Joyce Grenfell, who tells a story, as told to her by Virginia Graham Thesiger, a neighbour of Bebe and Ben's: "When Ben returned from some of his overseas missions he was to be seen on the doorstep of Southwick Street giving away lemons or possibly bananas to passers-by, who hadn't seen such rarities for a long time. They were good neighbours, particularly in air raids. Always helpful."

With the blitz in 1940, mounds of rubble in towns and cities grew where once buildings had stood. The war raged on.

To walk down London's Regent Street from Broadcasting House after a sleepless night of bombing was like coming across the Marie Celeste. The grey light shrouded the streets with an eerie stillness. Night had lost its power to silence the day. Silence only came with the dawn. Even London sparrows that might have gone flying off into the morning had been frightened away by the night's bombing. An acrid smell hung in the air of dying ashes from fires that had lit the night skies with hellish red and orange flames. American commentator Ed Murrow, in his broadcasts to North America, described these nights as 'London Is Burning'. In the dawn, not a sound; nobody to be seen. One knew where people were. They were in air raid shelters or down in the Underground trying to sleep on platforms.

This was the London that Bebe Daniels and Ben Lyon chose rather than the safety of America. Soon, though, their country would be engulfed in this war.

December 7, 1941. Out of the skies waves of Japanese aircraft appeared and bombed the American fleet at anchor in Pearl Harbour. The Americans, unprepared for the attack, reeled under the onslaught as Pearl Harbour lay in a conflagration of fire and ruin. This 'act of aggression' culminated in America's total involvement in the war.

American servicemen began arriving in Britain. As well as broadcasting in 'Hi Gang!', Bebe and Ben started another programme 'Stars and Stripes in Britain', specially beamed coast to coast in America over the Mutual broadcasting network. Through this programme, American families heard the voices of their menfolk in Britain. And with other British and American stars, they helped to form the American Overseas Artists Unit which travelled Britain entertaining the forces. They were also appearing in *Gangway* at the London Palladium, one of the shows produced by theatrical people to help dispel wartime blues with songs, music, dancing, glamorous girls and costumes. *Gangway* closed on 14 December 1942. The day after, 15 December 1942, Ben enlisted. He was sworn in and commissioned major in the U.S. 8th Army Air Force, commanded by General Ira Eaker.

As American servicemen, women and G.I.s arrived in Britain, we welcomed them and got accustomed to being stopped in a London street to be asked, "Pardon me ma'am – can you tell me the way to Licester Square?" (Leicester Square) or "Buckin*gham* Palace?" Clubs were opened throughout Britain. One of these had been in existence since 1940. It must be remembered that many Americans volunteered for combat service, particularly with the R.A.F., before America came into the war. Cecil Madden recalls:

"In November 1940 a group of Americans in London got together to found a Club to be called the American Eagle Club in London. On Thanksgiving Day on behalf of the B.B.C., I produced a radio programme when General Wade Hayes and Quentin Reynolds spoke. The premises were in Charing Cross Road which had been badly blitzed. The Club was opened with a big broadcast with Vic Oliver, Bebe Daniels and Ben Lyon, Carroll Gibbons, Claire Luce, Dorothy Dickson and Nat D. Ayer who played his own great songs, 'If You Were The Only Girl In The World' and 'Oh, You Beautiful Doll' with Bebe singing. At my suggestion the B.B.C. continued the programme weekly in its North American Service. It never missed a week for five whole years.

"The programme soon moved to a basement in Shaftesbury Avenue run by the American Red Cross called 'Rainbow Corner'. It was rebroadcast by the Mutual Broadcasting System, the Don Lee Network and many other stations.

"When Major Glenn Miller came over for the Allied Expeditionary Forces programme, he at once offered me the dance band of the A.E.F. conducted by Roy McKinley.

"After D-Day, I inserted a highly valued feature every week called 'Purple Heart Corner' in which Bebe Daniels interviewed wounded from the Normandy Front. A listener wrote to me, 'When Bebe Daniels went into that hospital, just about everybody in the U.S. went through with her.'

"My old friend Ben Lyon, then a Colonel, became so enthusiastic about Bebe's weekly spot that he suggested she should go to the U.S. hospitals on the Italian Front. Within hours she was flown there in her battledress. That night she wandered about the forward troop positions in her usual friendly way and nearly got captured by the Italians for her pains. That would have been a story for the Press! Later, Ben rang me. 'You know something?' he said, 'we nearly lost Bebe!'

"In a closing programme Phillips Carlin of the Mutual Broadcasting System spoke to us across the Atlantic and brought on a Mr Wells, a parent who had officially believed his son dead until months later he heard Bebe Daniels interviewing his son in our programme. Both he and his son sent us greetings in the closing stint.

"This Club alone gave shelter and entertainment to many thousands of American servicemen. Imagine how much more Bebe Daniels was able to give to many millions of families back at home."

24

Here's Wishing You Well Again

After the war started and with the inevitable increase in the number of sick and wounded, I talked with Cecil Madden, my chief and Head of the B.B.C. Overseas Entertainment Unit, about a programme for forces in hospitals. Cecil said, "Go ahead — think up something good." He gave it the title: 'Here's Wishing You Well Again'. Noel Gay wrote the signature tune.

We asked Howard Agg: 'How do you like the idea?" He liked it. Howard was also a producer in Cecil Madden's unit which was broadcasting programmes twenty-four hours

A moment of concentration before going on the air with Bebe introducing Clark Gable in 'Stars and Stripes in Britain'. With them are (left) Sergt. Kenneth Hulse from Perkins, Oklahoma, and (right) Sergt. Roscoe Grisham, from Oak Grove, Louisiana.
(*B.B.C. Copyright photograph*)

Bebe on the Normandy battlefront, recording messages with two wounded American servicemen for the B.B.C. overseas radio programme 'Purple Heart Corner' beamed coast to coast across America by the Mutual Broadcasting System and Don Lee network.

The London they loved. Bebe and Ben with Barbara and Richard against the background of the Houses of Parliament – taken soon after they returned to London after the war.

Royal Command Performance. Bebe and Ben are presented to H.M. The Queen (now H.M. The Queen Mother).

Bebe and Jill Allgood sign their book *282 Ways of Making a Salad* at the Army and Navy Stores in London. Also in the picture is Thomas Joy, then the store's book buyer.

'Can Bebe come out to play?' Bebe plays cricket with young friends from Cambridge Square, round the corner from the Lyons' house in Southwick Street.

'Life With The Lyons'—Scenes from the television programmes

(*top*) Bebe, Ben and Richard with Florrie (Doris Rogers), their larger-than-life neighbour in the programmes, (*centre*) Ben scoring a point over his 'boss' (Hugh Morton) to Bebe's amusement and a shocked Aggie (Molly Weir), the Lyons' 'housekeeper', (*bottom*) Barbara has fallen in love with a Texas cowboy (Arthur Hill). She listens ecstatically as he embarks on twenty verses of a Western song, 'Oh, Bury Me Not On The Lone Prairie'. By the tenth verse Bebe and Ben wonder – how many more?

round the clock in the Pacific, Eastern, African and North American Services. Together, Howard Agg and I devised and produced 'Here's Wishing You Well Again'. The programme started in the Overseas Service and was later also heard in Britain. For most of the war it came from the Criterion Theatre in London's Piccadilly Circus, taken over by the B.B.C. as one of its wartime studios — moderately safe as it was underground. Towards the end of the war it moved to the Paris Cinema, home of 'Hi Gang!'

Along with Mantovani and his Orchestra and Rita Williams, the resident singer, we had competitions on an unprecedented scale in the B.B.C. with money prizes; also a wishing well. Wishes from the forces were granted from the 'well' to hear familiar sounds from home, favourite songs, guest personalities, stars, and so on. Bebe and Ben, still broadcasting in 'Hi Gang!', were often requested guests on 'Here's Wishing You Well Again'. This was where I first met them.

After Ben joined the U.S. 8th Army Air Force in 1942, 'Hi Gang!' came to an end. Bebe continued with her broadcasts from the American Eagle Club and 'Stars and Stripes in Britain'; and she co-starred with Max Wall, Richard Hearne, and Claude Hulbert in a musical show at London's Piccadilly Theatre, *Panama Hattie*, presented by impressario Lee Ephraigm. Bebe played the exotic Hattie Malone. It was one of the successful wartime shows, filling theatres every night with civilian audiences escaping briefly from the terrible realities of war, and with British and American forces in London before they went to war.

One night the theatre was badly damaged by a bomb which hit the neighbouring Regent Palace Hotel. Fortunately the show was over and the theatre was empty. So *Panama Hattie* went on tour until another London theatre, the Adelphi, became available. It continued at the Adelphi until, for safety reasons, places of entertainment had to close.

Ben would recall, "An air force crew who had been to the show and went round backstage to say 'hullo' to Bebe afterwards, named their Boeing 17 bomber 'Bebe's boys'."

'Hi Gang!'; the American Eagle Club; 'Stars and Stripes in Britain'; *Haw-Haw*; *Gangway*; *Panama Hattie* . . . One newspaper said of her, "We in Britain thought Bebe was the best part of Lend Lease."

I felt, knowing her so well from her guest appearances in 'Here's Wishing You Well Again', she would be an ideal hostess for the programme. Her gay and vivacious personality would be a tonic for the sick and wounded. But it was a pretty big *if* with her other commitments. I asked Cecil Madden — what did he think?

"Excellent," he said, "if you can get her . . . but *Panama Hattie* is a big production for a start. Anyway, why don't you ring her?"

I rang her at the theatre. "Come round," she said. "We'll talk it over."

In her dressing room as we talked, we were constantly interrupted by Bebe being called on stage through an intercom. I remember her putting on a high, extravagantly decorated hat; then the intercom demanded she was wanted on stage. Taking a last look at herself in a mirror, she smiled. "We can't talk here. Why don't you come round for supper?"

I went round to 18 Southwick Street. We talked far into the night. Bebe didn't hesitate. She said, "Yes," and she stayed with the programme for most of the duration. Sometimes we worked during the day on scripts, sometimes at night, depending whether Bebe had a matinée as well as an evening show in *Panama Hattie*. On what we called our 'night shift', and with my day's work finished in the studios, I would go along to 18 Southwick Street and sit down on the steps in the blackout to wait for Bebe to arrive from the theatre. There was no point in ringing the doorbell or shouting down the area steps, although I knew that Ada the cook was in the kitchen. Ada was rather deaf, but I could hear kitchen noises, so it was comforting to know she was in the house.

Then I would see two pin-pricks of light coming across Cambridge Square into Southwick Street. It was the taxi bringing Bebe home. Taxi and car lights were hooded in the blackout; only pin-pricks of light were allowed. She would jump out of the taxi with a bright and cheerful, "Hullo honey . . . oh, it's a shame you waiting outside like this . . ." I would assure her that after being in an underground studio all day, it was good to sit out in the open for a while.

There was always a nice warm feeling going into 18

Southwick Street, the house with the blue door. Ada usually sensed our coming in rather than hearing us, or she could hear Bebe's vibrant voice calling her.

However serious the moment in the bombing, laughter was never far away. We thought up plenty to bring laughter and gaiety as well as all kinds of interesting people and subjects into 'Here's Wishing You Well Again'. Sounds from home included anything from fish and chips frying in a fish shop or a Hyde Park orator, the Dagenham Girl Pipers or the Hampden Roar (the famous roar of the crowd at the Scottish football stadium). Stars who took part included Margaret Lockwood, Joyce Grenfell, Arthur Askey, Vic Oliver, Anna Neagle, Jessie Matthews, Jack Warner, Elsie and Doris Waters, Beatrice Lillie, Robert Donat, Ann Shelton, Yvonne Arnaud, Cyril Fletcher, Adele Dixon, Stanley Holloway, John Clements, Flanagan and Allan, Vera Lynn, Emlyn Williams, Harry Hemsley ... so many others; sportsmen like Gordon Richards, Len Harvey, Joe Davis, Henry Cotton, Sir Malcolm Campbell, Bruce Woodcock, Graham Walker; and B.B.C. personalities like Freddie Grisewood, Leslie Mitchell, John Snagge, Alvar Liddell, Marjorie Anderson (of 'Woman's Hour' fame). Marjorie Anderson compèred 'Here's Wishing You Well Again' when it first started. J.B. Priestley and Malcolm Sargent were also guests.

Sonia, Lady Melchett, recalls some of her memories of Bebe and Ben. As Sonia Graham before her marriage, Lady Melchett worked with me on the production of 'Here's Wishing You Well Again'.

"I remember Bebe vividly. She was a dynamic personality and a true professional – always full of good humour and wisecracks – a real life enhancer. As well as stars and personalities we had amateurs on the programme, like a London flower seller or a country farmer. The forces in hospitals used to ask to hear from all sorts of people. We would give them scripts to study while Mantovani and his orchestra were getting ready, as well as all the things that go on in the engineers' control room before a show. After a while I would notice the amateurs were much more interested in what was going on in the studio than in their scripts, whereas Bebe was going through hers word for word. We were constantly having to bring the amateurs back to their scripts! Bebe would help with this because she knew how important it was to be really familiar with a script before you went on the air. I learnt a great deal from her about being 'professional'.

"Bebe really brought the programme to life and I'm sure her vitality and zest must have communicated itself to the men in hospitals. We had a terrific fan mail from all over the world. I remember two middle-aged ladies – we called them Doc and Doris – coped with the fan mail; they did nothing else full time. Bebe personally answered her mail and we often wondered how she did it all. She was in *Panama Hattie* and had other broadcasts to North America. I can never recall her being late. I always felt she was a dedicated person, giving much so willingly.

"Occasionally Ben came to London on a snatched forty-eight-hour leave, and would appear at the studio and watch the show. In spite of the fact that at the time I was in a teenage state of total self-absorbtion, I remember thinking that theirs was a marriage to be admired. Although they had completely individual and separate identities, they were very much Bebe *and* Ben."

Max Wall remembers:

"My personal reactions about these charming people are, in retrospect, that they were, and I suppose that Ben still is – the right kind of folks.

"Bebe was a kind of disciple of show business, inasmuch as she was dedicated to it, and possessed the infinite capacity for taking pains to achieve – these, I am told, are the qualities of a genius.

"She, I believe, was the motive force behind all the scripts written for their radio shows, and very successful they were.

"She was also a lovely person to know, full of vitality and charm, warm and affectionate. I can recall many jolly times at the old Olivellis' in Store Street off Tottenham Court Road, where the 'Pros' once gathered together for the purpose of Italian food and laughs, and camaraderie – after the show, wherever it was, Olivellis was a must.

"Evidence of Bebe's thoroughness lay in the fact that her singing teacher Laurie was always in evidence, and Bebe made a practise of going through every song in *Panama Hattie before* the show opened each performance.

"When Ben got any leave and came to the theatre, I recall that he looked very smart in his American Air Force uniform."

Eileen Hunter, who appeared in the Home Guard concert at Buckingham Palace, recalls another occasion:

"After an opening night – if I remember it was *Panama Hattie* – a supper had been arranged in one of the hotels. Bebe arrived looking as fresh as an orchid with no trace of theatre make-up. She didn't keep anyone waiting. She was wearing a beautiful orange chiffon gown and she looked stunning. I said to her, 'How have you done it . . . after a first night?'

"She smiled, 'Oh, I've been home and had a bath and put on fresh make-up.'

"I thought then — what a girl! She must have done it all in about thirty minutes flat. But that was Bebe. She never appeared anywhere unless she was immaculately groomed and dressed, and I believe she timed these things down to the last minute."

One day during the run of 'Here's Wishing You Well Again', working with Bebe in 18 Southwick Street, I sensed something was wrong. She was unusually quiet and thoughtful.

"Everything all right?" I asked her.

"Oh sure . . . fine," she replied. But I could see by her expression it wasn't. I did not press the point. She would tell me if she wanted to. A couple of days later, Ben arrived home unexpectedly. He strode into the dining-room where we were working.

"Darling," he began, and broke off to say a brief "Hi, Jill" to me, crossed to Bebe, and put a piece of paper on her table. "Darling, look at this!"

Bebe raised her eyebrows and glanced at the piece of paper. "I've seen it."

I disappeared. Whatever "it" was, they were best left alone.

Later they told me what it was all about. General Ira C. Eaker, Commanding General of the U.S. 8th Air Force, sent Captain Jock Whitney and Colonel Ben Lyon to Washington to present to General Hap Arnold, Commanding General of all U.S. Air Forces, and his staff a film which would show them the necessity for the continuance of American precision daylight bombing on enemy-occupied territory. After this presentation and discussion, both Captain Whitney and Colonel Lyon were given two weeks' leave in order to visit their relatives and friends before returning to Europe.

Ben was the house guest of Louella Parsons and her husband Dr Harry Martin during his stay on the coast and a party was given each night for him. The first three nights Louella arranged for Norma Shearer to be Ben's partner as they had started their careers together as extras in New York. For the fourth night Louella invited as Ben's partner an up and coming singer named Gail Robins as she thought people would misconstrue – make something out of Ben's being seen only with Norma Shearer. Ben was introduced to Miss Robins and they spent the evening together in the company of thirty other guests. On the way home, Louella, Dr Martin and Ben dropped Gail Robins off at her house. Ben thanked Gail for a lovely evening and never saw her again.

Several days later the late Hedda Hopper, another American columnist who was a rival of Louella Parsons, printed the following in her column: "While Bebe Daniels is ducking bombs in London, Ben Lyon is seen nightly in the company of Gail Robins. A divorce is imminent." This was the first and only time the term 'divorce' was associated with the names of Bebe Daniels and Ben Lyon.

The story was sent to Bebe in London. Too shattered and heartbroken, Bebe made no attempt to get in touch with Ben to verify the story, thinking there must be some truth in it, otherwise it would never have been written, and she felt her marriage was going to break up. Ben was unable to get in touch with her because censorship would not permit him to telephone London from America. So he got special permission and rushed back to London on the first available plane. He explained it all to Bebe – that this item had been written by a jealous rival of Louella Parsons.

Before Ben left California he confronted Hedda Hopper and demanded a retraction, threatening legal action.

"I was surprised to hear from her, she had written it thinking it would hurt Louella Parsons personally, since Bebe and I were Louella's closest friends. I said in front of a group of people – if ever she printed an article like that again I would slap her across the face."

No one had ever talked to Hedda Hopper in this way. Bebe and Ben were never mentioned in her column again.

So it ended happily. Ben went back to war. Bebe carried on in London.

D-Day and the Normandy invasion – 6 June 1944. On D-Day plus 15, Ben flew Bebe to Normandy – the first woman civilian to join the invasion forces. Here she recorded reassuring and cheerful interviews and messages home with the American wounded 600 yards behind the front line, showing the speed and efficiency of the chain of evacuation. For this and her war work in Britain, the President of the United States approved her being awarded the Medal of Freedom, America's highest civilian decoration, which is only awarded for heroic services in circumstances of extreme danger. The same medal was awarded to the lunarnauts of Apollo 13.

Bebe's citation reads:

Bebe Daniels Lyon, American Civilian, for exceptionally meritorious achievement which aided the United States in the prosecution of the war against the enemy in Continental Europe, from 16 December 1941 to 26 May 1945. During this period she distinguished herself by her initiative and unfailing interest in the welfare of the American soldier. With outstanding ability she organized, produced and acted in theatrical productions presented to civilians and troops and was the first woman civilian to follow troops in the Normandy landing in order to record wounded American soldiers 600 yards behind the front line. Her unselfish service and willing sacrifice under the most dangerous conditions contributed immeasurably to the maintenance of a high state of morale among the troops, thus materially contributing to the success of the war effort.

At the same ceremony Ben received the Legion of Merit. His citation read:

Lieutenant-Colonel Ben B. Lyon honorably served in active Federal Service in the Army of the United States from 15th December 1942 to 9th October 1945.
    Legion of Merit awarded 9th December 1946 at March Field, California, to Ben B. Lyon... [by Lieutenant-General Ira C. Eaker] ... World War II Victory Medal issued at Los Angeles on 7th November 1947.

After the liberation of Paris in 1944, Ben had to go to one of the notorious German concentration camps. Bebe went with him. She was deeply affected and saddened by what she saw — the gas chambers, the ovens and stinking huts; corpses being dug up to be reburied with dignity; and, in her words, "relatives of the dead laying their pathetic little bunches of flowers near the gas chambers, the ovens and outside the huts and on the graves."

At the end of the war, in a special B.B.C. radio programme, Bebe interviewed Sir Alexander Fleming, the "bacteriologist at St Mary's", whose discovery of penicillin had saved millions of lives. Sir Alexander was an extremely modest man about his work and achievements and he would never talk about himself. Particularly, nobody could persuade him to appear on radio. Bebe was in fact the person who finally persuaded him. This episode is told by André Maurois in his biography of Sir Alexander Fleming.

"In July 1944 the newspapers published the new Honours list. The 'bacteriologist at St. Mary's had become Sir Alexander Fleming, and his wife, Lady Fleming . . .'

"The investiture took place in the Palace basement, for security reasons.

"In the following year, 1945, Sir Alexander planned a tour of the U.S.A.

" 'I have the impression,' writes Dr. Clegg (a colleague), 'that few people realise what a magnificent ambassador for Britain Fleming was when he went abroad. Modest to the point of shyness, by no means an orator on public occasions, he impressed those he met with his simplicity and essential humility . . .'

" 'I hear you are going to the U.S.A.,' I said to him.

" 'Yes,' he said, 'isn't it great? I am going to see the Brooklyn Dodgers.'

"Before leaving for America, he was, as befitted his new eminence, interviewed for the B.B.C. by Bebe Daniels. 'I had asked the B.B.C.,' she says, 'whether I could have Sir Alexander Fleming. Their answer was: "Oh no! Sir Alexander will never consent to speak on the radio!"

" 'All the same, I'm going to give him a ring."

" 'Sir Alexander never answers the telephone."

" 'I thought that rather odd,' continued Bebe, 'so I wrote him a letter and had it delivered at the hospital by my secretary, Joan Murray, with strict orders to give it to Sir Alexander in person. When she came back, I asked her: 'Well, what happened?'

" 'I was shown in to Sir Alexander and he said: 'Why all this fuss? Who sent you? Mr. Churchill'? 'No,' I answered, 'Bebe Daniels.' " She left my letter with him, and half an hour later Sir Alexander himself rang me up: "Come and see me tomorrow, at one o'clock, at St. Mary's."

" 'I was punctual to the minute. I had expected to find twenty-four secretaries, eight guards and I don't know what else. Actually, the only person I saw was a technician in a white overall in one of the corridors. I asked him: "Where shall I find Sir Alexander Fleming?"

" 'At the end of the passage: he's making tea."

" 'I found him with his sleeves rolled up, making tea over a Bunsen burner. "Would you like a cup?" he asked me, and, before I could say yes or no, I had a cup in my hand. Then he said: "It would interest me to talk on the radio . . . Would you like to see the original culture?"

" 'That'd be marvellous!"

" 'He vanished behind a pile of dishes, found the precious culture, and showed it to me. Then he asked: "What's the programme? What d'you want me to say?"

" 'You will be free to say exactly what you like, sir."

" 'I thought that'd be your answer . . . Here's what I've prepared." He read it to me, and it was perfect. Sir Alexander was marvellous, and had a delicious sense of humour.'

"In June, July and August 1945 Sir Alexander made a triumphal progress through the United States."

After the war this tribute to Bebe Daniels and Ben Lyon was broadcast by His Excellency The American Ambassador in London, Mr. John Hay Whitney.

"I am glad to add my few words about these two fellow Americans. Not only because I've known and admired them personally — there is another reason and this reason is, that in their own way Bebe Daniels and Ben Lyon have helped more than most people to strengthen the goodwill between America and Britain.

"You have heard how they elected to stay with you in Britain during the war. In those days, as I very well remember, their home in London was a haven for American Servicemen. They made us all welcome, from Boss General Ira Eaker right down the line and especially including Captain Whitney.

"I know that General Eaker found in our friends the

Lyons the only true relaxation he permitted himself from the tremendous load of responsibility he had to face at that time, and further, the hospitality they gave all of us was remarkable, as an enormous number of people can testify.

"I had the pleasure of serving with Ben Lyon on General Eaker's staff both in London and in Italy and I recall how Bebe Daniels, having been the first civilian woman to record the voices of the troops who had been wounded in the invasion of Europe, went to Italy to perform a similar service for our men there. In this work she never spared herself. It was a real dedication.

"When the war ended most of us Americans went home, but loving this country as they did, Bebe Daniels and Ben Lyon stayed. They had shared some grim days with you, days and nights of great trial and I am sure it seemed as natural to them as it has obviously seemed to you that they should continue to make their home in London. By doing so they continued to persuade their friends in both countries to think more kindly of each other.

"I send them both my good wishes."

At last, with the war in Europe over, Bebe and Ben began making plans to go back to their home in California to rejoin their children.

Before Bebe returned to America, she came up from the kitchen in 18 Southwick Street one day and said to me, "Jill, we must do a salad book." With rationing, salads had not been part of the British menu and they seemed to be limited to lettuce, cucumber, beetroot, tomatoes and so on, whereas salads were a major part of the American meal.

"You grow some of the best vegetables in the world," she said, "so why not use them in salads?"

We worked out ideas. Bebe would ask American stars and personalities to contribute recipes and I would do the same thing in Britain. We would also create our own recipes. The title was *282 Ways of Making a Salad* — an incredible thought at the time that there could be so many. On both sides of the Atlantic, everyone we asked responded enthusiastically and the cover of the book read:

Here are the favourite salad
recipes of

Sir Laurence Olivier	Vivien Leigh
Bing Crosby	Betty Grable
Michael Wilding	Jean Simmons
Tyrone Power	Greer Garson
Strube	Anna Neagle
Gregory Peck	Dorothy Lamour
Jimmy Edwards	Margaret Lockwood
Walter Pidgeon	Betty Hutton
John Mills	Kay Stammers
Alan Ladd	Judy Garland
Richard Dimbleby	Susan Hayward
Denis Compton	Gene Tierney
Van Johnson	Googie Withers
Bob Hope	Diana Wynyard
Robert Donat	Joan Bennett
Norman Hartnell	Elsie & Doris Waters
Vic Oliver	Joan Crawford
Stewart MacPherson	Valerie Hobson
Donald Peers	Veronica Lake
Richard Widmark	Joy Nichols
Sid Field	Linda Darnell
Humphrey Bogart	Yvonne Arnaud
Ted Ray	June Haver
Frank Sinatra	Anona Winn
Wilfrid Pickles	Rosalind Russell

And Many Other Personalities and Stars

282 Ways of Making a Salad became an Anglo-American
effort to create a book. Britain would be rationed for several
years, so looking at the book now there are some odd
references like, "If bananas are not available" or "If cream is
not available, use recipe for mock cream".

Bebe sent me ideas from America and when she returned
to Britain she was armed with more ideas. We then completed
the book together. Every recipe was made and tested. In later
years, Barbara said, "No wonder I don't like salads — I had to
taste all theirs." To our knowledge it was the first book of its
kind to be published in this country and, when the first
edition appeared in 1950, it was heralded by the Press as a
much-needed book after the years of rationing. Bebe's
inscription bore this out:

I dedicate my part of '282 Ways of Making a Salad' to those unsung heroines the British housewives who, at last, can get some of the tools with which to do the job.

A second edition followed in 1953. In America it was published under the title, *The Complete Book of Salads*.

From 29 August to 9 September 1950, London had its first British Food Fair at Olympia. The General Organizer, George H. Grimaldi, asked Bebe and me if we would have a stand at the Fair with our book and salads on show. Every night we made fresh salads for display the next day. Bebe's mother and my mother helped, and early the next morning we all took the salads down to the stand. Ben, Barbara and Richard came along as often as they could, and stars who had contributed came as well. But perhaps the great story of this Fair was that the British hadn't seen anything like it for so many years. Thousands flocked to Olympia. Sometimes it looked like a sea of people coming along the aisles looking at the things they had been deprived of for so long.

Bebe and I were also asked by the National Farmers Union to support stands and tents at their country shows, where vegetables and fruit in serrated ranks were on display. One boggled at what we could grow.

Bebe would say jubilantly, "You see what I mean!" – and we made even more salads to show.

25

Return to America

New York was exciting and exhausting when Bebe and Ben stopped over on their way back to California to look up a few friends and Ben's family who had come from Baltimore to meet them. Florence Foster, a close friend, was in New York at the time. Her husband, Harry Foster, was Bebe and Ben's agent in Britain for many years. Florence Foster recalls: "Everybody wanted to give them parties and newspaper men wanted stories. Their telephone never stopped ringing. They laughed in their good-humoured way, 'It's wonderful,' they said, 'but,' Bebe added, 'I think we'll have to go back to London for some peace and quiet!' "

It was all pretty overwhelming for these two war-entrenched people emerging into the limelight of New York before their friends finally let them go back to California.

But in family re-unions two people were missing. Little Mother and Ben's brother Edwin died during the war.

Margot Grahame looks back: "After the war when Bebe came back to Hollywood, she asked me one day to have lunch with her to celebrate the fact that she was going to produce her first film for Hal Roach. 'I'm going to write and produce it,' she said. She was very excited. I remember we were having pancakes, American style, with maple syrup and crisp bacon. Anyway, when I asked her what the film was about, she laughed and said, 'About a talking dog.' It was the kind of story Bebe loved . . . a dog getting a girl in and out of scrapes.

"It was a lovely part for a woman. Assuming it was already cast, I said, 'Lucky her.'

"Bebe replied, 'Yes, aren't you?' She laughed again – that lovely laugh of hers."

That was how Margot Grahame came to star in the film *The Fabulous Joe*. From then on Margot, Bebe and Ben became great friends.

"On Sundays, Ben used to come and collect me. I spent most Sundays with them in their beautiful Santa Monica home – and oh, those lovely luncheon parties! Everybody seemed to be there – Douglas Fairbanks, Mary Pickford, Reginald Gardiner . . . I can't tell you . . . Louella Parsons. Such gay talk! We'd have fried chicken Southern style, corn on the cob, salad . . .

"Then they returned to England. Ben was made Casting Director, I remember, for Twentieth Century-Fox in London, so I didn't see them for some time, until I came to England. I rang them up and I can hear their voices now: 'Margot! When did you get in? Darling . . . Come on over!' And over I went to 18 Southwick Street.

"I had to go back to America, but I finally came to live in London."

Margot Grahame settled in London when she married S.D. Peters, the celebrated literary agent. "And of course living in

London meant I could see a lot more of Bebe and Ben again, which I did. They used to come and have dinner with us. But I suppose I remember Dolphin Square most vividly, where Bebe and Ben lived in the last few years of Bebe's life. I used to go over for dinner. Ben was a wonderful cook. Like most American men, he loved cooking and he used to make marvellous meals.

"One evening, Bebe and I were talking about salads – she was a great girl for salads – and I happened to say, 'I love a Caesar salad.' Bebe called out to Ben – he was busy taking a look at what was going on in the kitchen – 'Oh Ben, what about a Caesar salad? Margot loves a Caesar salad.' Now, if anybody knows anything about a Caesar salad, they will know it can take two or three hours to make.

"Ben called back, 'Does she now? Well, Margot's not having a Caesar salad – she's having just what I'm serving her.'

"He was so houseproud. I can see him now after dinner getting out the roller broom to roll over the carpet just in case there was a crumb or two on it.

"Now mind your feet, Mommie,' he'd say to Bebe.

"She would raise her feet. 'Okay, Daddy, they're out of the way.'

Actually, I think he got out the roller broom to play with Skeeter, their poodle. Skeeter used to race round the room with Ben, having a high old game attacking the broom. Lovely, lovely homely scenes. How I loved to be part of it all. Then we'd settle down in the living-room and talk and talk . . . gab's the American word.

"Sad to think it's all over – and can never be repeated . . ."

Max Wall recalls:

"Ben Lyon was a good friend to me whilst I was in Hollywood in 1948. He was then Casting Director for Twentieth Century-Fox, and he procured for me, through the auspices of Eddie Pola, at that time my brother-in-law, a film test for that company – who offered me a seven-year contract that I turned down for various reasons. I can recall, too, performing for Ben and his associates a private showing of my popular Professor Walloffski act at the piano, in a huge studio on the Twentieth Century lot – they all enjoyed it immensely. It is a long time since I have seen Ben. I remember Bebe and Ben well, and with affection."

26

. . . And Marilyn Monroe

Much has been written about Marilyn Monroe, but perhaps it is not so well known that Ben Lyon discovered her. On 22 July 1958, *The Atlanta Journal and Constitution Magazine*, in an article written by Actor Cordell, Jr., reported:

> *Norma Jean walked into the office of*
> *Ben Lyon, Atlanta-born star and . . .*

HE NAMED HER
MARILYN MONROE

Would the world's most famous Marilyn still be a photographers' model named Norma Jean if it hadn't been for Ben Lyon, Atlanta-born screen idol of the 1920s and '30s?

True, Norma Jean was doing pretty well as a model and might have become a movie star anyway. But the Marilyn Monroe the world knows today probably would not have existed, as such, if Norma Jean Dougherty had not met the former Atlantian.

It was Ben Lyon who put together the names *Marilyn* and *Monroe* — the magic combination that was to define the glamour goddess of the generation.

Here's what Marilyn herself had to say to Lyon:

"You found me, named me and believed in me when no one else did. My love and thanks forever . . ."

She wrote that message on a photograph of the two of them. The picture is a treasured keepsake at 18 Southwick St. in London, England — the current address of Ben Lyon and his wife, Bebe Daniels, onetime Hollywood movie queen. . . .

Ben Lyon first met Norma Jean Baker Dougherty in the summer of 1947. He was head of casting at 20th Century-Fox Studios — and she walked into his office unheralded. But he knew immediately that she was a potential star. . . . .

"From the moment that Norma Jean Dougherty walked into my office," Lyon recalled recently, "I was certain she had star qualities. She came in at 11 a.m. — and within one hour I signed her to a seven-year optional contract, starting at $125 a week. At 6 p.m. that day, we tested her in color, and within a week exercised our option on her services.

"She was the most conscientious youngster signed by the company. She devoted all her time to study, training and exercise so that when an opportunity came she would be prepared. I have the greatest admiration for her."

Lyon created one of the world's most-talked-about names by adding *Monroe*, the maiden name of Norma Jean's mother (who was born Gladys Monroe) to *Marilyn*, a name for which he had a sentimental attachment. It seems that Norma Jean reminded him of the late Marilyn Miller, the Broadway musical comedy star of the 1920s, in addition to Jean Harlow. Marilyn Miller once co-starred with Lyon in a movie. . . .

It was a coincidence that Marilyn's married name actually became Marilyn Miller some years later — when she wed playwright Arthur Miller.

Lyon had great faith in Marilyn from the beginning, a representative of his former studio headquarters in Hollywood said. "He helped her get roles," he added, "no matter how small."

After Lyon was named assistant chief of productions for 20th Century-Fox in London, he heard little of Marilyn Monroe for several years. Then, like everybody else, he heard a lot about her. By 1954, when he visited the States and looked up his former protege on a movie set, she was Marilyn Monroe in the fullest sense of the words.

It was then, seven years after she had first walked up to his desk, that Marilyn autographed that photograph with her words of appreciation: "You found me, named me and believed in me when no one else did. My love and thanks forever." . . .

The latest Monroe-Lyon reunion took place last year when Marilyn was in England making a movie — and she spent an evening with Ben and Bebe. They recalled the day when Lyon first signed her to a studio contract.

Norma Jean Dougherty, a successful model whose face appeared on five magazines in one month before she sought a movie career, might have won stardom without that push from Ben Lyon. Who knows? But it was Ben, the former Atlanta boy, who first said *Marilyn Monroe.*

27

"Life With The Lyons"

The remembered joy of rushing home to listen to Bebe Daniels and Ben Lyon is still with me — it is part of my treasured memory bank.

Edward Woodward

Bebe and Ben returned to Britain in 1948, Ben as Casting Executive for Twentieth Century-Fox in London. Some magnetic force also seemed to draw them back, like having seen someone you love through a serious illness and wanting to know how they were in convalescence. They could not get Britain out of their systems. They brought Barbara, Richard and Bebe's mother, Phyllis, with them. Friends got to know Phyllis as 'Bunny'. Barbara started this. When she was a baby beginning to talk, the nearest she got to 'grandma' was 'Bunny'. It stuck.

When the family arrived in London, they went back to 18 Southwick Street. The tall, thin house with the blue door was quiet and deserted, still full of wartime memories they had left behind when they returned to America. They soon set about making it home again. The British, still rebuilding shattered lives and cities, were delighted when Bebe and Ben came home; they wanted to hear them again on radio.

The B.B.C. asked them if they would do a new series of 'Hi Gang!' with Vic Oliver. On 18 February 1949, the show went on the air with this introduction in the *Radio Times* :

HI GANG! 1949
Vic Oliver   Bebe Daniels   Ben Lyon
Tonight at 8.30
February 18
Bebe, Ben and Vic say . . .
'Hello, Gang!'

'Hi Gang!' first came on the air one Sunday in May 1940. It ran all through that critical summer, helped to cheer millions of listeners during the blitz, and became one of the most popular wartime programmes. This week the three stars will be entertaining you again . . . in the same show.

'Hi Gang!' will be broadcast in all Home Services, except West, on

Friday evenings at 8.30 and will be repeated on the following Sunday in the Light Programme at 6.0 p.m.

(Courtesy: Natalie Oliver and The Editor, Radio Times)

While this was happening, Barbara and Richard were settling down to a new life in England after their lives in California. 18 Southwick Street, looking across to another row of identical houses on the other side of the street, was totally unlike the comparatively luxurious house and surroundings they had left in Santa Monica overlooking the Pacific Ocean. Barbara recalls:

"I didn't like it when I first came over here. I thought everything was old-fashioned . . . everything in the house was cream. I've hated cream ever since! Things go cream fast enough. Mother and daddy soon put it right of course. Mind you, it was so soon after the war. In America they didn't have a tenth of the hardships they had here during the war.

"You know, I would go into a shop and ask how much something was in real money! Then I was very surprised when I went back to America to do a show. I didn't like it a bit. Everybody seemed to be in such a hurry – and in so much of a hurry to make money. I couldn't wait to get back to England. And I heard myself in a shop over there saying, 'How much is it in *real* money?' – believe it or not! I had gotten so used to the pound. That's a terrible thing, anyway, to say in any country. But just like mother and daddy, I fell for the British. I can't explain it . . . it was something pretty nice."

As Barbara and Richard settled down in London, they learnt from Bebe and Ben that the English language was sometimes rather different as spoken by Americans. One day over lunch in 18 Southwick Street, Ben patiently told Richard, "Now listen son, you do not call a London police constable riding a bicycle a 'cop'." And Barbara, who had been shopping in a London store, came home saying she couldn't understand why nobody could tell her where the elevator was. "I found it easier when I learnt to say 'lift'," she recalls. If she went into a greengrocer's and asked for chicory and was given endive, Bebe had to explain, "In England, chicory is endive. In America, endive is chicory." And so on.

And the Lyon could roar — as Barbara discovered. "I was always getting into trouble with daddy. He would wait up for me. Mother would go to bed or be writing, and there was this figure in a dressing gown in the hall waiting for me because I was late coming in. Daddy's voice could carry . . . *demanding* to know where I had been before I shut the door. I imagined all the windows shooting up in Southwick Street and the neighbours looking out and saying, 'That Barbara's late again!' "

Bebe and Ben laughed about it together, and in their active minds the family situations built up into an idea. When 'Hi Gang!' finished its run, they said, "Why don't we do a family show on radio — we've got a ready-made family."

Barbara was studying at R.A.D.A. (The Royal Academy of Dramatic Art), so she was ready to take part in any venture with her parents. In America, Richard had made films, including *Anna and the King of Siam, The Great Lover* with Bob Hope, *The Boy With The Green Hair, The Tender Years*, and *The Tree of Liberty*, so he was a competent young actor.

The title came easily: 'Life With The Lyons'. It would be situation comedy, based to a great extent on their own lives but larger than life. Both Bebe and Ben were masters of situation comedy. Britain was still shovelling up rubble left behind by Nazi bombers. She needed to laugh and join in with the folks next door who became the Lyons — the family they could recognize.

Pat Hillyard, head of B.B.C. Light Entertainment, liked the idea. The B.B.C. accepted it. So began one of the most popular and successful shows on radio and television. 'Life With The Lyons' ran for twelve years, from 1951 to 1963, only with breaks for holidays. Altogether there were nearly three hundred programmes. Of how much 'Life With The Lyons' was based on their own lives, Richard recalls:

"It was us, but a little crazier. Mother was vague at times and she was gay . . . sometimes sentimental . . . always the lovable mother. 'Pop', as I called him, told us what to do and it often backfired. On the programme he would say things like, 'What idiot did that?' and I would reply innocently, 'You did, Pop.'

"Barbara and her boyfriends came into it. If Pop and I threatened to embarrass her, she would curl up and say, "If you do, I'll die – I'll just die.' This became a catch-phrase. And Barbara was always asking mother, 'Can I borrow that dress or coat?' . . . or something else.

"It was true – I *did* come in and go out of the house, slamming the door. My father was always blowing his top. 'Don't slam the door,' he'd say, 'the whole house shakes.' For a while I'd remember to shut the door quietly – then nobody knew whether I was in or out! Mother would call, 'Is Richard in?' – and someone would answer, 'I haven't heard him go out.' Of course I'd forget, slam the door, and the whole thing started over again."

In real life, Richard dashed up and down the stairs. So was born the idea on the programme of Richard rushing up and down the stairs (helped with recordings) in a matter of seconds to fetch something, and Ben's "What kept you, son?" This became a running gag. Audiences loved it and many young boys in their homes tried to do the same thing, often substituting sliding down banisters, with disastrous results to their pants, to see how fast they could get downstairs.

One story revolved round a real cradle. It was Barbara's when she was a baby. When Richard and Angela's children Penny and Timothy arrived, the cradle was brought out and renovated with silk and frills – all the usual things for new-born babies.

The story in the programme was that Barbara wanted the cradle brought down from the attic. Bebe and Ben assumed she wanted it because she was going to have a baby. It was an hilarious programme with Bebe and Ben going out buying baby clothes and Ben going overboard buying toys and so on . . . only to discover in the end that Barbara wanted the cradle for a puppy.

At this period, Barbara was married to television producer Russell Turner. Their wedding in 1956 was an event of the London season. "But it didn't work out," said Barbara. "When the marriage was breaking up and I saw myself breaking up, mother and daddy were wonderful. They were most upset about it and they saw me through it all."

On 14 December 1968, Barbara married Colin Burkitt, an accountant. "With Colin," says Barbara, "I've found happiness. He's a darling. Mother thought so too — and Colin adored her."

Barbara and Colin's baby boy, Bruce, was born in May 1971. And Barbara had the famous cradle for Bruce.

"Richard," she said, "made it rockable . . . it took him all night. We had a nanny for a few weeks and when she saw that it was rockable she said, 'We can't have *this*!' That was the end of the rockable cradle."

"I had to stop it from rocking," added Richard. "That took another night."

So many incidents in 'Life With The Lyons' were based on real life, like Ben's *Hell's Angels*. This became a family joke.

"Did you really see me in *Hell's Angels*?" he would ask; then the inevitable let-down for him, assuming a hurt 'I can take it' air.

Bebe never grew older than thirty-two! When she was asked, "How long have you been thirty-two?", she would reply, "Well, I was never good at figures. But Ben says for twenty-five years."

'Life With The Lyons' began and continued with permanent characters like Florrie (Doris Rogers), their larger than life neighbour whom Ben constantly insulted and Florrie insulted him; Aggie (Molly Weir), their Scottish housekeeper/cook, a stalwart member of the family, a confidant in trouble, who helped to put things right when they went wrong; Mr Wimple (the late Horace Percival) and his 'wife' (Gwen Lewis) and their large and ever-increasing imaginary family of children. Mr Wimple's tummy often rumbled at embarrassing moments. This idea was born from a rumbling cistern at 18 Southwick Street.

Other characters came into the programme. Ben's boss (played by Hugh Morton), with whom Ben was usually more in trouble than out; David Enders who 'owned' shops like a milliner's or a florist's, Wilfrid Brambell occasionally played parts. In one programme in which he appeared, Bebe met Florrie at a country cattle auction. When she saw Florrie, she waved to her. The auctioneer thought Bebe was bidding for a Jersey cow. Bebe thought she had got a woolly jersey. Wilfrid Brambell delivered the cow (a real one on the television programme) to the Lyon house — and many complications followed with the family trying to hide it from Ben.

'Life With The Lyons' was situation comedy at its best. They found and kept to a successful formula.

"Part of the strength of our show," said Ben, "lies in the fact that we're always topical – and human. And we're sticking to that approach."

Bebe was the brains behind the programme as well as writing. Ben contributed ideas; but, as he says himself, he was not a writer. Bob Block was Bebe's main co-writer, although in the early years Bill Harding, a Canadian, contributed to the programme. When Bill went back to Canada and joined the Canadian Broadcasting Corporation, he was followed by Ronnie Hanbury.

Bebe had her own proved method of compiling scripts. She would work out a format of, say, six scenes with a 'curtain' at the end of each scene. Paul Fenoulhet and the B.B.C. Variety Orchestra bridged the scenes with appropriate music. I worked with her on ideas and stories and compiling an extensive library of sequences and gags. We could turn up gags on any subject. After each summer recess we tried to get programmes in hand, but somehow this never worked out. We always found ourselves working on the current programme far into the night. We never kept any record of how many dawn choruses we heard. Many writers find they do their best work after midnight. It has something to do with the quietness that settles – there are no daytime distractions. Asked once when she did her best work, Bebe replied, "At night when the dogs have stopped walking around and leaving the doors open, and all the radios are off."

Bob Block has his memories: "Bebe and Ben were in London at the time. I think it was soon after they came back from America. Derek Glynne was my agent – he heard they were looking for scripts, and he had some scripts of mine and Bill Harding's. He sent them to Bebe and she liked them. She asked to see us and it all started from there. The first thing we did with her was to collaborate on the script for a film with Hermione Baddeley – called *Hermoine's Hamburger Heaven*. Bebe was producing films at that time, I think for Hal Roach, and this was one of them. And later we started 'Life With The Lyons'.

"One thing I always remember was that I learned a lot from Bebe and Ben about comedy because they were both true professionals and they had a professional approach to comedy — they knew all the basic ground rules. This was so important because I didn't know a lot about comedy writing when we started 'Life With The Lyons' and I gained more and more knowledge. Bebe helped me greatly. She was always a patient person, she never got bad-tempered or anything like that, she was the type of person who was generous in passing on knowledge. She would also listen to your point of view too. It was a process of give and take. If you had a point to make she would change things. She always tried to be honest about what she was writing and certainly she thought if something had to be a certain way she held out for that.

The personal side I also remember about Life With The Lyons. Because it went on for so long — twelve years of radio and television — my children partly grew up with it. I remember . . . every Christmas there would be a present from Auntie Bebe and Uncle Ben when they were small. By the end of the series they were all getting big and starting to branch out for themselves. This applied to a lot of people who listened as well . . . millions of families all over the country. They started off as young people . . . young children . . . and it was more than a decade later that the series finished. So in a way they grew up with the Lyon family because the stories used to change in character . . . Barbara and Richard were getting older . . . Barbara getting married . . . Richard getting married and so on. In a sense people were watching the Lyons grow up as well.

"Was Bebe vague? Everybody is vague at certain times. Vagueness is simply the fact that you're trying to think of two things at once and your mind's not quite on one of those things. I think with Bebe she had this vagueness more than other people because she was always trying to think of two things at once, sometimes three things at once, but it was a delightful vagueness which we played on in 'Life With The Lyons', making her a gay, lovable person which without doubt she was."

Jean Hutton remembers: "I was Bebe and Ben's private

secretary for thirteen years and they were thirteen unforgettable years. When you work for the Lyon family, you are not just an employee. You become part of their warm family circle, and you are drawn in to all their activities like celebrating birthdays and anniversaries, meeting their friends and relations at dinner parties, etc.

"Bebe was a wonderful person to have as a friend. She was the only woman I know who could keep a secret. You could tell her anything in confidence and she would never tell a soul.

"She was also one of the most generous persons I have known. You dare not admire anything of hers otherwise she would insist on your having it.

"In the days when Bebe and Ben lived in Southwick Street, Bebe's office was down in the basement next to the kitchen. Everyone referred to her office as the salt mine. She would disappear down there and not be seen again for hours and hours. She and her writers used to work all through the night, and I would be upstairs in my little office waiting to type the draft. She was a perfectionist and would spend two or three hours on a few lines to get them right, and she could outwork any of us.

"Bebe was always very anxious to get the reactions of various people to the scripts, so we used to tick them for laughs. If we thought a particular line would get a laugh, we would tick that line — we all had different coloured ticks. I used to take a copy of the script home each week so that my family could add their ticks, and anyone who came to the house was pressganged into reading the draft and ticking it for laughs. The milkman was delayed on his round more than once!

"Christmas was a very special time of year with the Lyon family. Bebe had an almost childlike delight in Christmas, firmly believing in Santa Claus. She and her writers used to work like trojans getting extra scripts written so that Bebe could have time off to go shopping and prepare for Christmas. She used to make long lists of family and friends, including all the pets. I was continually finding scraps of paper in all sorts of places where she had made out a Christmas list.

"Life With The Lyons"

"Bebe and Ben gave presents to every child in the neighbourhood. It was a mammoth task finding out their names and ages. Bebe was very particular about getting the right presents. The house in Southwick Street was knee deep in bulky Christmas parcels, and I was on my knees every day wrapping and labelling them.

"Ben would not show much interest until Christmas Eve when he would be caught up in the excitement; then he would disappear for a couple of hours and do his own shopping. It was always his job to trim the tree. After he had finished it, we had to stand and admire his handiwork. It looked beautiful every year. And the family pets weren't left out. They had presents under the tree — so did friends' pets!"

Tom Ronald was their producer throughout the radio series. John Phillips and Joan Kemp-Welch produced television programmes. For realism, sets were created by designers Frederic Pussy and Bernard Goodwin to be as near as possible to the Lyons' actual home — so the family really felt they were at home in television studios.

Molly Weir writes: "One of my most vivid memories of the hundreds of shows we did was a night at Wembley T.V. studios. Jack Buchanan was our guest star, and it was to be our final show before we all broke for the summer holidays. We'd been rehearsing from 10 a.m. as usual, the audience were assembled, and we were all ready to go just before 8 p.m. after the usual 'warm-up' to get the audience in a good receptive stage for the show when — all the cameras broke down! It was a technical hitch of gigantic proportions, it seemed. But of course, knowing nothing of the innards of cameras or the intricacies of temperamental 'parts', we blithely assumed it would right itself in a very short time.

"Ben went out and did a few gags to keep everybody amused. Bebe called to me, 'Come on Aggie, you can do something', so I roped her in and we did a take-off of the Beverley Sisters singing, 'Sisters, sisters, there were never such devoted sisters'. The audience lapped this up, and called for more. We followed this with 'I Belong to Glasgow', and then checked the cameras again. Nothing doing.

"The audience by now were convinced they were watching a variety show and began calling out requests. 'Maybe It's

Because I'm a Londoner', they yelled insistently. I found this absolutely hilarious. There we were, Bebe and I, one an American and the other a Scot, strolling back and forth like Flanagan and Allen singing in pseudo-Cockney the much beloved war-time song, and the audience joining in as though the whole thing was part of the expected show.

"Meantime, Jack Buchanan waited patiently in his dressing room. It was now coming up to 10.30 p.m. I knew what dedicated professionals the Lyons were, and I also knew that holiday plans would prevent any postponement to a later date.

"The canteen was re-opened, and crates of orange juice and ginger pop passed round the audience, and fresh sandwiches and biscuits handed round to keep body and soul together. Some were getting distracted about trains, others about baby-sitters, and it was vital for the success of the performance that we kept them with us, but short of locking the doors, what else could we do to amuse them?

"Community singing kept everybody happy for the next half-hour, especially when they could clap with 'Deep In The Heart of Texas'! Barbara and I did a little dance. Bebe and I went out again and fooled around. Ben told more stories.

'The technicians got those cameras right at well after midnight, and at 1.15 a.m. we recorded the last scene. We'd arrived at Wembley at 9 o'clock the previous morning! And for all those who think actors live the life of Reilly, this was all taken as an 'act of God' and the word 'overtime' wasn't even *mentioned*.

"This is only one of many memories which so enlivened the years I spent as one of the Lyons' family. For I *was* regarded as part of the family by the public, who thought I lived with them, and nothing I could say would convince them otherwise. In the end I gave it up and just agreed that I was indeed their friend and housekeeper, and lived with them in their very own house. It made those who wished to think this way happy that they could picture us all together during the week, living out the life which entertained the public for twelve glorious years. When one thinks of the number of hours of entertainment pouring from radio and television seven days a week, it is a tremendous tribute to the Lyons' popularity and appeal that the public still remember the shows with lasting affection."

Doris Roger recalls: "It was the focal point of one's life – going to rehearsals. The first rehearsals always started on a Tuesday. I so looked forward to it all every week, and wondering what the stories were going to be – how much Ben would insult me or how much I would insult him. Quite often after the show, people in the audience would say, "You got your own back on him tonight, didn't you?"

"I remember one television show. We had a chimp in it. During the actual show, Bebe, Barbara and I had to wear furs – we were going somewhere special. We didn't put on the furs until the final rehearsal and the chimp got furious. I don't think he thought we were one of them. I don't know what he thought. Anyway, we had to abandon the furs and just wear our dresses. And if I remember, he nipped one of Ben's fingers, not seriously, but Ben kept his distance for the rest of the show.

"After Bebe was ill and I'd go into a shop, people would say, 'I saw you on television last night' . . . then immediately, 'How's Bebe?' I missed it all so much, working with Bebe and Ben. They were such darlings and such fun – so was everyone else."

At one period, families from bombed-out parts of London were moved into houses in Cambridge Square, round the corner from Southwick Street. One day the doorbell rang. Whoever was nearest the door always answered it with a, "I'll get it." On this day, I opened the door. Standing on the step were about six small boys from Cambridge Square. They were carrying a cricket bat, stumps, and a ball.

"Can Bebe come out to play?" asked one of them.

"Can you go out to play?" I called to Bebe.

She dropped what she was doing and went out – to play cricket with them in the Square garden.

"I've never played cricket in my life," she said. "They put me into bat and by a fluke I swiped the first ball way over the trees."

The boys cheered and hailed her as *the* cricketer of their set. "But I knew I couldn't repeat it and that would have been a terrible let-down," laughed Bebe, "so I insisted on giving the bat to one of the boys."

More than an hour later, Ben went round to the garden to see what had happened to her. "There she was, fielding in the slips or wherever she was supposed to be, having the time of her life."

Apart from working on the scripts, there were rehearsals, clothes to get ready (changes of clothes in television), hairdressing – all that goes with a star appearing before an audience. And then the show itself, when she must be 'on top'. Bebe was always on top. She seemed able to outstrip anyone in the race of keeping going.

Ben recalls, "Friends used to come over for dinner and to play Canasta. Bebe would go on after dinner writing the script. We might have two tables of cards going in the living room. By about two o'clock in the morning the folks would begin to pack up, and suddenly Bebe would appear bright and cheerful, 'Who's going to play cards with me?' Everyone was ready to go home to bed and Bebe was all ready to play cards, but none of us had the heart to refuse her. This was her one relaxation from the endless hours of work."

Two films of 'Life With They Lyons' were made, directed by Val Guest. One of these, *The Lyons in Paris* took the family and cast to Paris. And a stage show was produced in Blackpool, again with those 'permanents' – Molly Weir, Doris Rogers, Horace Percival and the others, as well as actresses and actors including Diana Dors, Philip Ashley, Alan Barclay, Peaches la Rue, Jill Fenson, Ray Buckingham, and Sheila Bernette. The show was presented by Tom Arnold by arrangement with Jack Taylor.

During summer breaks, Bebe and Ben took holidays in the South of France and Majorca. But over the years since their return to Britain, there were many demands on their time. They made personal appearances in theatres round the country. They opened fetes and appeared in charity shows. On 27 November 1959, the *Marylebone Mercury* reported: "Comedian Ben Lyon set two hundred people rocking with laughter when he opened a Christmas Market in aid of the St. Marylebone Housing Association Building Fund ... 'I haven't spent any money yet,' he said, 'but if anyone is interested, Bebe is for sale.' " Sam Costa was also there on that occasion helping to raise funds.

May Goldsmith, a long-standing friend, organized a 'Bebe and Ben' club. The club did a great deal of work through its members for charity. For instance, Bebe and Ben endowed for life two cots in a children's hospital. And such was their popularity that two white rhinos at London's Zoo were named after them!

They became active members of The Variety Artists' Benevolent Fund and S.O.S. (Stars' Organisation for Spastics). Ben was a member of The Water Rats; Bebe a member of The Lady Ratlings — both organizations made up of show-business people who do a great deal of work for charity. Both were members of Equity, and Bebe was a member of the Society of Authors, the Screenwriters' Guild of America and its British equivalent, The Writers' Guild of Great Britain, and A.C.T.T. (Association of Cinematograph, Television and Allied Technicians).

Altogether Bebe and Ben appeared in seven Royal Command Performances, with stars like Anne Neagle, Jack Hulbert and Cicely Courtneidge, Joyce Grenfell, Stanley Lupino, Adele Dixon, Bobby Howes, Leslie Henson, Florence Desmond, Evelyn Laye, Beatrice Lillie, Bud Flanagan, Ches Allen, Nervo and Knox, Anne Ziegler and Webster Booth, Margaret Leighton, Vic Oliver, Margaret Lockwood and a host of other stars who appeared in these Royal Command shows.

Margaret Lockwood writes: "I knew Bebe and Ben and met them often socially. What I remember most is a train journey up north — at the time of Irene Dunne's film *The Mudlark* in which she played Queen Victoria, to stage a repeat in Manchester of the Royal Command Film Performance and, during the journey, Bebe and Ben taught me how to play Canasta."

The Mudlark was one of the films for which Ben was responsible in the casting, including Andrew Ray, the son of Ted Ray, as the boy star — the mudlark.

And so it continued year after year, but Bebe and Ben would not have had it otherwise.

"If," Bebe once said, "if I had my life all over again, I wouldn't want to miss one minute of it ... I would want to do the same things all over again."

Angela, Richard's wife, has her memories: "When Richard

and I became engaged, Bebe paid me the biggest compliment anyone could pay. She said, 'If Richard had asked me to go out and find him a wife, I would have picked you.' I always thought that was a lovely thing to say." Richard and Angela were married on 1 July 1961. Their children, Penny and Timothy, "made us proud grandparents," said Bebe and Ben. "They are lovely children — at least we think so."

On 20 February 1959, Bebe's mother died in London. Bebe wrote this tribute to her:

OUR BUNNY

As twilight drew a soft curtain over the sky and stopped to wait for night — God reached down and gently gathered our Bunny to His arms like a sleeping child. For one brief moment she opened her eyes and saw what we could not see — a glimpse of where God had taken her. For Bunny was truly a child of God and she died as beautifully as she had lived.

Bunny was a rare person who never said an unkind word about anyone in her life. She bore no malice nor hated any man.

She was natural . . . She was friendly . . . She had profound wisdom and great charm . . . She was fun . . . She was gay . . . She was the kind of person you met for the first time and yet felt you had known all your life. She was intelligent and interesting and comfortable to be with, to talk to and listen to — whether you were young or old, godly or wordly — because Bunny loved people and understood them and saw goodness in the worst.

When you were in trouble, hers was the voice you wanted to hear. You were never afraid to tell her your innermost thoughts, and she never betrayed a confidence. She was always there when you needed her. Her love for others was her purpose in life. She helped to keep your vision clear and gave you strength and moral courage. Somehow Bunny could always find sunshine in the darkness.

Bunny was a rare person. She walked through life with a firm step. Her road was broad and sunlit and she feared no winds that blew.

She loved God and all things of beauty and Nature. She was never in too much of a hurry to stop and admire a lovely blossom . . . a tree . . . or a blue sky.

When I was a child she taught me how to find pictures in the clouds and to see beauty in a weed. She pointed out the colours in the rainbow and drew enchanting pictures in the sand. She taught me to fear no man as much as myself. She showed me how to make friends with small wild creatures. Once she picked up a small wounded bird from the road and took it home and nursed it until it was well enough to fly away.

I remember how she could never rest if she thought an animal was hungry or a flower was out of water.

Her heart was always doing beautiful things and she gave freely of all she had.

Bunny was a rare person. .Her friends were legion and she was greatly loved. The twilight of her passing lies heavy in our hearts . . . for we will never see her face again or hear her voice on Earth. But she has left us rich in all things that matter . . . and one thing is certain — as long as someone can see goodness in the worst, find sunshine in the darkness, comfort a friend . . . As long as someone stops to admire a lovely blossom, a tree, or a blue sky . . . As long as someone cannot rest while a flower is out of water or a tiny bird needs help — Bunny will live. Please God keep her vision clear.

Her daughter,
Bebe.

*These are the thoughts of her family
and all her friends.*

When 18 Southwick Street was due to be torn down, Bebe and Ben moved to a modern Georgian-style house in Abbotsbury Road, Kensington, "where we had a garden for the first time," they said. Bebe grew roses; Ben mowed the lawn and dug flower beds. Bebe used to count her roses, saying ecstatically to friends, "We've got nearly two hundred," — or whatever number there were. And for a long time, as Ben dug the borders, a robin followed him round. If he stopped and rested on his spade, the robin hopped on it. "And there I had to stand," he would say, "not daring to move until he decided to hop down again."

They created another busy home in Abbotsbury Road; 'Life With The Lyons' went on.

28

' This Is Your Life '

During one break in 'Life With The Lyons', Bebe and Ben returned to America for a visit. While they were in Hollywood a TV company planned Bebe's 'This Is Your Life'. Ben and Louella Parsons helped in a major way, but they had to do it secretly so as not to arouse Bebe's suspicions. This led to all sorts of complications, with Ben receiving and making strange telephone calls and having clandestine meetings with people. Bebe just didn't know what was going on. In the end, "I got very suspicious of what Ben was up to."

If Bebe answered the telephone and it was a woman's voice, the woman hung up. Once, when she came into the room, Ben was speaking softly into the phone with his hand cupped over the mouthpiece; but she caught the end of the conversation — "Can you make it for lunch darling? Okay — I'll be right over."

"Who was that?" she asked brightly.

"Oh . . . business. I have to go now." He kissed her goodbye. "See you later mommie."

Bebe watched him go. Business! . . . darling!! . . . whispering down the telephone!!!

If Ben wasn't on hand, "and I got to the phone before our secretary answered it," Bebe would recall, "if it was that same woman, she always hung up." The 'woman' was a studio secretary, but she dare not say who she was.

To cap it all, Barbara and Richard, who were being flown from England for the programme, missed the plane, "because," Barbara recalls, "it was booked from over here and they booked it in English time — they didn't allow for the change from the east coast, New York, to the west coast, California. Of course, I was always late, but I never missed a plane. We went on time on the schedule we got from the airplane people — and I was never allowed to live that down! But we nearly gave the game away because the airline people phoned mother and daddy in California and said, 'Your daughter and son had to get on the next plane.' Mother almost answered the phone — it was just luck she didn't. Her secretary answered it and *she* had a few awkward moments with that call. I dread to think what would have happened if mother had answered it! But thank goodness she didn't."

Finally everything was arranged. Bebe and Ben were sent a formal invitation to the studio. A few hours before the show, Ben had a few bad moments when Bebe said to him, "You know, darling, I've been in so many studios, I think I'd rather stay home and watch the programme on television than go out this evening."

For a few seconds Ben was shocked into silence, but he

thought fast. Bebe was making no attempt to get dressed. With no time to lose, he said, "Now listen, sweetheart. I'm going to let you into a secret. I shouldn't tell you, I know, but they are going to do Louella's life tonight and they will probably want you to make a brief appearance."

That was enough for Bebe. "Why didn't you tell me in the first place?!"

"Oh honey — you know how these things are — you're not supposed to tell anyone."

There was no time for further explanations. "Bebe got ready so fast," said Ben.

In the studio theatre they sat with Louella and her husband. The programme went on the air. Ralph Edwards, the host and compère, introduced it from the stage; then he came down into the audience to where Bebe, Ben, Louella and her husband were sitting. He introduced Bebe and Ben. The audience, obviously delighted to see them, gave them a tremendous round of applause.

(Ralph Edwards presented Bebe and Ben with a filmed copy of the programme. When they returned to London, Ben ran it in their home for friends. I recall it well.)

After introducing Bebe and Ben, Ralph Edwards turned to Louella and her husband. Bebe smiled and looked rather knowingly at Louella as Ralph Edwards talked with her. From the comments he was making you could see, in her mind, Bebe thought he was coming up to the announcement: "Louella Parsons — This Is Your Life!" But for a second or two he switched back to Ben and Bebe. He was saying something to her; then he announced: "Bebe Daniels Lyon — This Is Your Life!" Bebe's expression, the beaming smile for Louella, changed to utter disbelief. The audience applauded madly as Ralph Edwards took her arm and led her to the stage. Through the applause you could hear her saying, "But they will have forgotten me . . . it's been so long . . . we've been away so long," and Ralph Edwards replying, "They haven't forgotten."

As he led her to the stage, he turned to the audience. "Give her a big hand, she's trembling a little," and turning back to Bebe, he asked her, "Are you all right?" She was obviously very moved as she nodded to him.

So began the life story of Bebe Daniels on American TV.

Those who appeared were Harold Lloyd, Hal Roach, Cecil B. de Mille, Louella Parsons, Ben, Bebe's mother, Barbara and Richard, a British air raid warden, an American mother who had lost two sons in the war whom Bebe had interviewed, and Harold Pinto, the sculptor, who told his story of how Bebe took him into 18 Southwick Street when he was badly injured outside the house in an air raid.

When Harold Lloyd was asked by Ralph Edwards, "What did you think of Bebe when you and Hal Roach first met her all those years ago, when you signed her up to be your leading lady?" – Harold Lloyd replied, "We liked her . . . Oh yes, we *liked her*." Harold Lloyd heard for the first time that Bebe had given him the nickname 'Speedy'.

Ben told how he finally won Bebe – and she quipped back, "How do you know I didn't fix the whole thing!"

In his tribute to her, Cecil B. de Mille said: "I have watched your useful life from the first day you came into my office wearing a suit borrowed from your mother. You thought you had gotten away with it. Maybe you did. Remember what I said to you? Next time you come and see me, don't wear your mother's clothes. Within six months of joining me you were no longer a comic star – [he corrected himself – a comedienne – you were a dramatic star and you more than justified the faith Jesse Lasky and I had in you. I am very happy to have had some part in your brilliant career and inspiring life. God Bless you, my dear."

Back in London, Bebe opened a business in Kensington High Street, specializing in Victoriana and other periods, and in interior decorating and furnishing, with a modern fabric section. Lamps were another speciality, all attractively displayed. The business, under the joint names of Bebe Daniels – Richard Lyon, was not so much for herself, but for Richard – to give him a more secure future than show business might one day offer. From her Hollywood days she had studied antiques and decor. Period film sets have to be accurate in such details.

We all got roped in. Richard, Ben, Barbara, Babs Hillyard and I went with her all over the place to buy antiques. Jean Hutton helped to run the shop. Richard studied the business, working long hours to make it a success. Bebe was in her element, spending as much time as she could from her work on 'Life With The Lyons', meeting people, advising and passing on her knowledge.

She found time somewhere to write a series of articles for the *News of the World* on interior decorating and replying to letters from readers asking for advice. But as time went on and with each season's return of 'Life With The Lyons', Ben became worried. He knew Bebe was overdoing things. Once, when she went down with flu, her doctor – Dr Goldman – warned her against overworking. She had been warned about overworking in Hollywood. Now she was doing the same thing in England.

But some inner force seemed to drive her on. One day in May 1963 without warning, she collapsed in the shop with a cerebral haemorrhage and was not expected to live. Fortunately, Ben was in the shop at the time.

"Dr Goldman saved her life," he said afterwards.

From nearby St Mary Abbots Hospital where the ambulance took her, Dr Goldman had Bebe transferred to the National Hospital, Queen's Square. There, with the constant vigilance of doctors and nurses, she gradually recovered. Ben spent days and nights in the waiting room and at Bebe's bedside – hardly leaving the hospital unless the children and friends insisted he go out for a meal. Vyvienne Moynihan, now an executive in the Central Office of Information, was one of their friends who kept vigil with him – and of course Barbara and Richard were constantly there. Hundreds of flowers arrived from people, known and unknown; a bouquet arrived with a card simply inscribed, "From the taxi drivers of London". The whole country was anxious. Prayers were said in churches. Papers printed her progress. One day a placard read: BEBE LATEST.

Recovery was slow, but at last Bebe was able to return home, Ben her constant companion. At first she had a day and night nurse; then as she continued to progress, a day nurse. She had to learn to walk all over again, with the help of her doctors and Mr Faer, her physiotherapist and his masseuse, 'Margie' as we knew her. Ben poured courage into Bebe, spending hours with the nurse from those first few hesitant steps, walking her. "And," he would say, "*she* had plenty of courage . . . I knew she would beat it."

29

About Religion

The Lyons were neither saints nor sinners. They simply had certain standards of ethics and morals by which they lived, and they talked freely about religion. In telling his background, Ben said, "I was brought up in four faiths. My father was Methodist, my mother part Jewish and until I was three I was raised in the Jewish faith. Then my father insisted I become a Methodist. When my mother became seriously ill she joined the Christian Science Church and I became a Christian Scientist also. But all that changed. Bebe being a devout Catholic, I felt I should enter the Church so that our family could share the same faith."

Father Carmine de Felici was Bebe and Ben's priest for many years. He first met them in 1939 through Tony Reddin. Although Ben did not become a Roman Catholic until some time later, Bebe attended Father de Felici's Church, Our Lady of Dolours in Hendon, for several years.

Father de Felici was appointed priest of St Edward the Confessor Church, Golders Green, London, in December 1962. He takes up the story:

"It may come as a surprise to those who know Bebe and Ben — because they did not wear their religion like a badge on the lapel of their coats — that they were deeply religious. I myself discovered this one Good Friday when Ben rang me up and he said to me, 'A happy Good Friday, Rabbi' . . . and I was busy trying to work up an idea for a sermon. I never write out sermons and I never write out speeches because I have always found — after forty years as a priest — it is always better to leave this to the inspiration of the moment. That Good Friday call was a case in point. I was getting frantic because time was drawing nearer for me to go up into the pulpit and I was still playing around with an idea. And then Ben phoned me . . . 'A happy Good Friday, Rabbi . . .'

"I was furious – for the first time in my life I was furious with Ben. I said somewhat bitterly, 'Ben, that is hardly in good taste.'

"Ben replied, 'I thought my news would make you happy.'

"I asked, 'What news?'

" 'I have just decided to become a Catholic.'

"I was amazed and replied, 'Ben, I can't talk at the moment . . .' I was too full.

"I went straight down to the church and found them looking for me because I was due to get up in that pulpit. I entered the pulpit and I said to them, 'This is the happiest Good Friday of my life.' I realized, like the words of Christ, 'If I be lifted up I will draw men to myself.'

"I must say with humility that I felt I never preached a better sermon in my life. I did not mention Bebe and Ben. I could not do that. But I waited patiently until that day when I received Ben into the Church.

"These were happy times – my instructing Ben, as I learnt a lot from him and his next-door neighbour Dr Harry Thornton, who also wanted to come into the Church. We started the instruction – or rather conversations – in Ben's room at 18 Southwick Street. We went down to the dining-room for lunch where we had a gathering of his family and script writers – and the conversation carried on across the table. It was not my wish, but they were all so enthusiastic. Later on I discovered how sincere Ben was – that if he went to any function he insisted on the Friday abstinence.

"On the day he was confirmed by the late Cardinal Griffin – the Cardinal liked Bebe and Ben so much that on the occasion of their silver wedding he graced the gathering with his presence, most unusual – the Cardinal was supposedly to have said privately, 'Ben posed a great theological problem – May a Bishop, even a Cardinal, confer a Sacrament of Confirmation on one of Hell's Angels delivered?'

"And what of Bebe? I have hardly referred to her in all this, but you may rest assured that many times Bebe said to me, 'I have prayed for this and now it has come true.'

"When Bebe and Ben were in *Gangway*, they sent me an

invitation for the opening night. I thought I couldn't get away to go, so I sent Bebe a telegram: 'Regret unavoidable absence but will be with you in prayer.'

"Back came a telephone call from Bebe: 'What do you mean – you will be with us in prayer! You will be right here with us when the curtain goes up.' I was.

"I used to go to the dressing room to see her in 'Life With The Lyons'. Someone would say to Ben, 'Hullo Ben, I didn't know there was a parson in the show.'

" 'What do you mean – parson? He's a priest – the real thing. He's come to see Bebe.' He would laugh and say to me, 'What's wrong Rabbi, couldn't you get a seat at the Windmill?'

"Ben would try stories on me to see if I would laugh, to get my reaction.

" 'What's the idea of telling me stories?' I would ask. And he would turn to whoever was there and say, 'To get a few stories for the programme, I pop down and see the Rabbi – bring them back and polish them up.'

"All this banter – how we all enjoyed it. And underneath it all, Ben was deeply religious and always he was respectful to his religion.

"When Bebe was seriously ill in 1963, Ben sent for me. As you know, many longs hours were spent at Bebe's bedside – and never for a moment did Ben lose faith. The start of those eight borrowed years really was at Bebe's bedside, and when Ben helped her out of the hospital and got her home where he always wanted her."

In November 1966, The Rev. Dewi Morgan, Rector of the Church of Saint Bride in London, asked Bebe if she would write her views about Christianity for a publication he was planning. Bebe wrote:

"I am one of the fortunate people in the world who knows the meaning and the power of prayer. I have always been a devout Catholic, attending Mass whenever it was possible.

"My family was a Roman Catholic family, so naturally I was baptised in the Catholic faith and brought up in all its beliefs. From childhood my associations with the Church have been very strong. I was educated in the Sacred Heart

Convent in Los Angeles, California, and one of my aunts was a Sacred Heart nun.

"As I grew up I found that Christianity in many forms became the only real way of life. I was never told I had to go to Church on Sundays. I went, not because I thought it my duty, but because I wanted to go and to take part in the Mass. But, at the same time, I learned that a Christian way of life isn't only in the Church. I have always enjoyed my life – whether in work or play. I like to have fun and to see other people enjoying themselves. I love to have my family and friends round me – young and old – and there is nothing I like better than a gay party. One of the things Christ said was, 'Be of good cheer'. Today he would probably have said, 'Have fun'. After all, He was the most cheerful of people.

"Throughout my life I have been grateful for the gifts which God gave me – to be able to sing and act and write. And I have been so grateful to have had so many opportunities to use these gifts in my work. I believe we are all given certain natural gifts – and it depends on us how we use these. Sometimes things do go wrong, and often one finds that in these circumstances people give up. This is one of the reasons I believe that faith and prayer mean so much.

"During each hour I have spent in the House of God I have prayed for my loved ones, my friends, my enemies and myself. Little did I know that one day, 23rd May 1963 to be exact, I would have such a serious illness that the last rites would be given to me and I would need the prayers of others. Friends and total strangers from every corner of the earth sent messages and prayed for my recovery. Novenas were made by complete strangers. My husband and family attended daily Masses and prayed by my bedside for days and weeks. God answered the prayers and today I have practically fully recovered. From a state of paralysis I am now able to walk up and down stairs, go to theatres, visit friends' homes, and I am writing again . . . So I am always puzzled when I hear someone say, 'I believe in God, but I haven't time to go to Church.' This to me is like saying, 'I love my mother, but I haven't time to go and see her.'

"I believe quite simply that faith in God and the power of prayers are the greatest part of the fulfilment of life. God has been extremely good to me and I thank Him with all my heart; and I shall spend the rest of my life trying to make up to Him for all He and the Blessed Virgin and her son Jesus and Saint Jude have done for me."

30

Eight Borrowed Years

Ben asked me if I would help in the antique shop. But however hard Richard, Jean Hutton and I worked, the odds built up against us.

"Rent and rates doubled, then trebled," said Ben. "We decided it wasn't worth going on. Why throw money away on rent and rates for a shop? We couldn't ask people to pay double or treble just like that – so we decided to close down."

Richard, already an experienced photographer, went into photography professionally.

Bebe continued to improve. As she recovered she always sat at a table beside a window in the living-room on the first floor of their house on Abbotsbury Road. Frankie Howerd, then a near neighbour, often came by.

"He would stop underneath the window," Bebe would recall, "wave up to me and give a gallant bow – and I always waved back. He made my day."

Frankie Howerd recalls: "Those days are among my more cherished memories. I used to go for walks in Holland Park opposite Bebe and Ben's house, to learn lines. Sometimes I would go in to see them for a chat. Bebe would say, 'How's my boy today?'

" 'Fine, I'm fine,' I would say, 'How are *you*?'

" 'All the better for seeing you, my dear,' she would reply.

"We chatted about everything. She wanted to know all the showbiz news – and what was I doing? Ben was always there. I believe he never went out unless he had to for something.

"I liked and admired Bebe and Ben so much. If in some way I was able to help make her day, Bebe made *mine* every time I passed that window and she waved — or when I went in for a chat with her and could see her gradually getting better and better."

"But," said Ben, "there comes a time in everyone's lives in a house when stairs are stairs." To make things easier for Bebe, they gave up the house in Abbotsbury Road and moved to a flat in Dolphin Square. For a time, Bebe still had a day nurse, Jan Towler. I used to go over for weekends. Bebe had always wanted to write mystery stories; she was now so well recovered she felt she would like to do some writing. Her doctor — Dr Ratner — agreed it would be a good idea for her to have this interest, so we started writing again, without pressure, and never in the evenings.

Then nursing ended. I now had no family ties and Bebe asked me if I would consider coming to live with them. I had been one of the family for so many years and she was convinced it would work. The relationship between Bebe, Ben and myself was perhaps unique. Bebe never had a sister, neither did I; so we were like sisters. Although I have two brothers, Ben was like a third brother to me.

We went for holidays in Antibes, South of France, and to Majorca, where Barbara and Colin joined us. Back in London, Bebe and I continued writing. Our first short story, 'The Heart Of The Matter' was published in the *Evening News* on 25 June 1969.

With Bebe's recovery, she and Ben enjoyed those evenings when friends came for supper and they played bridge or canasta, or we all went out, or just watched television. And there were birthdays and anniversaries to celebrate at home with family and friends.

Anne and Peter Goodall came often to play bridge. As Sports Editor of the *Evening Standard* and with a mutual interest in sport, Peter and Ben had a lot in common. As well as playing golf together with other friends like Harry Lipman and Bob Gross, Ben was a tennis and boxing fan. He followed Wimbledon, if time allowed, on television; and in the evenings from his ringside television seat, he spurred on champions like Henry Cooper and Muhammad Ali — as well as young amateurs. He explained the finer art of boxing to Bebe and me as we watched with half an eye while we played

Kalooki. We did learn, though, that amateurs wear vests in the ring.

Like 18 Southwick Street and the house on Abbotsbury Road, the flat in Dolphin Square was a magnet. It drew people from all over — friends who lived in and around London like Betty and Ben Russell; Sybil and John Coventry; Betty Harris; Blue Lyon (no relation — just the same name); Florence Foster; Babs and Pat Hillyard; Robin Hillyard; Barbara and Harry Levinson; Grace and Frank Owen; B.B.C. producer, Bill Worsley and his wife Betty; Norman and Phyllis Sterritt brought flowers from their show gardens in Symond's Yat in the Wye Valley. And friends came from America if they were staying or simply passing through London. Some were life-long friends like film producer 'T' Freeland and his wife June (formerly June Clyde); Foxy Leschin, Stephen Sondheim's mother; Harold Lloyd; composer Sam Coslow; Dorothy Treloar who, with Dorothy Manners, took over the Louella Parsons column in Hollywood; Sylvia Hecht, who went to school with Ben. And friends of friends who told them before they left the States, "Ring Bebe and Ben when you get to London." They rang and were welcomed with, "Come on over!"

The list was endless . . . I remember people coming at 5.30 for a cocktail and they were still there at 8.30! These were times to reminisce and be brought up to date with news on both sides of the Atlantic.

When Phyllis Diller and her husband Warde Donovan were passing through London in September 1970, Phyllis Diller wrote to Bebe and Ben afterwards from Los Angeles: "It was so nice to spend a little time with you in London. I have a feeling we could reminisce for a couple of hours."

And among all these names, what happened to Staff Nurse Kelly of the National Hospital, Queen's Square, who did so much for Bebe when she was in that hospital and who came to Dolphin Square to keep in touch? Where did Nurse Kelly go? We could never find out.

Bebe's first visit to the theatre with Ben after her illness was to see *Charlie Girl* at the Adelphi starring Anne Neagle. It was at the Adelphi that she had played in *Panama Hattie* way back in the wartime days. At the end of the show, Anna

Neagle spoke of her admiration for them, an admiration which was echoed in the hearts of millions. They were an inspiration to us all, she said, and she was proud and honoured to welcome them that night. Spontaneously, the whole audience gave Bebe and Ben a standing ovation. Their pleasure at seeing her smiling at them from a box, with Ben at her side, was unrestrained.

Writing in *The Silent Picture*, Summer/Autumn 1971, Dame Anna Neagle said: "I felt so flattered when Bebe chose to see *Charlie Girl* as her first outing after she had been so dangerously ill. When I announced her presence to the audience the reaction is something I shall long remember – a heartfelt tribute to a great person and trouper."

Later, they went to the London Palladium to see a show starring Ken Dodd. It was another evening of memory and nostalgia. On this stage they had made their first appearance in London in 1936, and had appeared in so many Royal Command Performances.

Bebe and Ben had been given the royal box where the night before Her Majesty the Queen, His Royal Highness Prince Philip and other members of the Royal Family had watched a galaxy of British and American stars at a Royal Command Performance, including Ken Dodd. Three other friends and I were with Bebe and Ben that night. At the end of his show Ken Dodd came down to the footlights. "Ladies and gentlemen," he said, "as you know last night we were honoured with the presence of Her Majesty the Queen . . . She sat in that box . . ." He pointed to the royal box. "Tonight we are honoured to have another queen with us – someone else we all love – a queen of the theatre and films, radio and television – Bebe Daniels! . . . and her husband Ben Lyon!"

Once again a vast London theatre audience rose to its feet. The applause and cheers grew to a crescendo, engulfing the now floodlit box like a great wave. And once again Bebe and Ben stood side by side, smiling their thanks. Yes, of course Bebe had tears; so did Ben; so did we all.

During these years Ben did quite a lot of broadcasting and television. And now people wanted to hear Bebe again. In the spring of 1970 the B.B.C. asked her if she would be the mystery voice in the radio programme 'Twenty Questions'. She agreed and it was a great success. Afterwards, when she went on to the studio stage, the audience gave her a wonderful reception. Robert Dougall, the television news reader, was also a guest that evening, and he was delighted to see her looking so marvellous and well.

Later, the B.B.C. invited Bebe to be the guest on another radio programme, 'Sounds Familiar'. As Jack Watson, the programme host, led her on to the stage the applause she received from the audience — suddenly they were all standing applauding — lasted a full twenty seconds.

Both programmes were broadcast from the stage of the Paris Cinema, home of 'Hi Gang!' and 'Life With The Lyons'.

Apart from these few public appearances spread over quite long periods, Bebe and Ben were perfectly content to spend their lives at home with their family and friends or visiting them; or, if they were on their own, watching television.

Angela remembers other occasions: "Whenever we went to see Bebe and Ben with the children, Bebe always did drawings with them, or played cards like 'Snap'. We always came away armed with sheets of paper — all the drawings they had done together. Penny and Timothy called her 'Bamba'. When Penny first started talking, the nearest she got to Grandma was 'Bamba', although they were always able to say 'Grandpa'. The children loved going to see Bebe and Ben, and of course *they* loved to spoil them, like all grandparents . . . something extra special for tea and a present to take home as well."

On the subject of drawings, a picture Bebe once painted hung in the living-room. "An early Daniels," she laughingly called it. Simplicity was the theme — two lighted candles; a white one in the foreground with a glowing flame, and a smaller black one in a more shadowy background with a dull flame. The picture represented good over evil.

Perlita Neilson recalls the first time she met Bebe and Ben at Dolphin Square: "They asked me to have tea with them. Oh, what *fun* they must have been to work with. Because it was *fun* to go to Dolphin Square and laugh and chat and have more tea. Particularly as at that time I was not working and actresses are always easily depressed when they have no part to play. Ben tried to help me all he could, and indeed I was glad, happy, to follow his advice on various very practical points.

"*Even* today I think I must get new photographs, as he recalled actresses who had visited him and didn't look *quite* the way they did seven years ago. And writing all necessary letters before embarking on a part which might show you to advantage – because by the time you begin rehearsals *that* is the only thing you think about.

"*Thank* you Bebe and Ben for asking me and for this memory of you both."

Thelma Holland, widow of Vyvyan Holland, recalls meeting Bebe and Ben in Dolphin Square:

"Years before, in Australia, I was a film fan of Garbo, Rudolph Valentino, and Bebe. Bebe for her vibrant personality. It was a thrill to meet both Bebe and Ben in London and to find – even after her illness – that her warmth and kindness was as I had 'felt' it through the cinema screen.

"Bebe and Ben were generous too, in many ways and to many people in all walks of life. Like all generous people they took a great interest in food and entertainment. One always had a sense of 'belonging' when one visited.

"Apart from being husband and wife and acting together they were good companions and once you met them you were their companion as well.

Bebe and I were sitting in Dolphin Square garden one summer day when Ethel Revnell came along carrying a bundle of scripts. "Well," she said, "fancy me seeing you today of all days. I've been turning out these scripts in the storeroom." She sat down with us and flipped over some pages. "Look at this . . ." showing us a page. "All these lines . . . Bebe, Ben, Ethel . . . takes you back a bit, doesn't it?"

Recalling that afternoon, Ethel Revnell said, "We had one of those lovely showbiz chats. Bebe always radiated warmth; you were immediately at home with her – just that warmth. And she had such a quick brain, full of ideas and she'd give you advice so willingly. I was very fond of them both, Bebe and Ben."

So many people came into Bebe and Ben's lives, "but," I

can hear them say, "let's not forget Muriel Hughes." A good friend, Muriel Hughes was always on hand when help was needed. She came from the North of England to live in London and we saw a lot of her in Dolphin Square. The flat echoed with laughter as, in her words, "I tried to teach Bebe and Ben some North country expressions like, *Have a tab* (cigarette); *Hoy it over!* (throw it over!); *I thaa why you're all stannin around* (I know why you're all standing around); *I'm gannin now* (I'm going now).

"Bebe used to say, 'If *Life With The Lyons* was on the air, I'd have someone like you in it as one of the characters.' Aye, they were a grand family and I still miss them."

31

A Few Raindrops Started to Fall

In the coming months, Bebe was her usual happy self. Those of us who were close to her could never have suspected that soon she would be stricken with another serious illness. Without warning she collapsed. Her doctor sent her back to the National Hospital, Queen's Square. Later, she was transferred to St Teresa's Hospital, Wimbledon, in the care of nursing nuns, to convalesce. We shall long remember The Reverend Mother Catherine; Sister Bernadine, the Matron; Sister Ignatius; all the nuns.

On her seventieth birthday, 14 January 1971, Bebe was still in St Teresa's Hospital. Eamonn Andrews, in his Thames Television 'Today' programme which she watched in her room, sent her a cheerful birthday message, not only from himself but from millions of people everywhere whom he knew wished her full recovery and many happy returns.

Ben and I went to the hospital every day, staying late into the evening. Barbara and Colin, Angela and Richard, were constant visitors and a few close friends were allowed to visit. Bebe seemed to make progress; we all had such high hopes for her recovery. Then the doctors said she could come home. On 6 February 1971, Ben's birthday, he brought her home. "The best and only birthday present I want," he said.

He did everything humanly possible for her, installing a special bed and equipment in the flat. "I don't care if I spend every penny I have," he said. He engaged a day and night nurse – Carol Chapple and Eileen Monahan. Cheerful, kind and efficient, neither of them watched the clock. They gave freely of their own time when it was needed.

Bebe fought back from this illness with the same courage and the same indestructible spirit. She still radiated happiness and warmth; she still had flashes of gaiety; she still loved people to come and see her. "How are you?" they would ask. "All the better for seeing you," was her invariable reply. The children came often. Close friends like Florence Foster and Natalie Oliver visited. Florence Foster sat quietly with her and they talked about the days of show business. When she was allowed to sit up, Natalie Oliver played backgammon with her. Lily Coyle, her masseuse, came often. One thing Bebe enjoyed eating – caramel custards. Lily Coyle made delicious caramel custards and she must have made many dozens for Bebe. Peter, her hairdresser, came to do her hair. I recall that Peter was dressed in his best suit specially for Bebe, although he knew it would get splashed.

But sometimes we felt a strange, chill feeling. She would say things like, "As we grow older and come nearer to death, time becomes more precious . . ."

The evening before Bebe died, she spoke to Florence Foster on the telephone. She told her, "I've been for a walk in a beautiful garden." Actually she had been dozing and had dreamt this, but she talked about that dream as if it really happened.

At five o'clock on the morning of 16 March 1971, Ben and I were with her as she passed peacefully and quietly away – into that beautiful garden of her dream, we liked to think.

Later, Dr Ratner said, "You must all be grateful – she really had eight years of borrowed time."

Tributes to Bebe in letters, telegrams and cables were legion from all over the world. World press, radio and television paid their tributes. The great respect which people held for her was epitomized in countless requests for Church Masses to be said for her in many countries – some for years;

some in perpetuity; her name is inscribed in the Golden Book of Liverpool Cathedral.

On Saturday, 20 March 1971, her personal friends and hundreds she had never met came with Ben and her family to mourn her in the Church of St Edward the Confessor, Golders Green, London. Father de Felici officiated at the service — Mass of the Angels. Anna Neagle and Richard Attenborough read the Lessons. In a moving address, Father de Felici said, "With the death of the beloved Bebe Daniels another chapter has been written in the story of life with the Lyons."

The day was cloudy and overcast with a cold wind. In the church, the service had reached the point of choir and congregation singing the hymn, 'Abide With Me'. On the line 'Through cloud and sunshine, Lord abide with me', the church was suddenly flooded with sunshine.

The sun continued to shine as we left the church and the cortège walked the short distance to Golders Green Crematorium chapel for the cremation service. After this service we came out of the chapel to a vista of hundreds of floral tributes lying on paths and lawns. And a few raindrops started to fall . . .

Newspaper placards that day read: LONDON SAYS FAREWELL TO BEBE.

Anthony Slide, Editor of *The Silent Picture*, wrote in the Spring 1971 issue this tribute to Bebe (Harold Lloyd died shortly before Bebe, on 8 March 1971):

"I had arranged to insert a brief note of the death of Harold Lloyd in this issue of *The Silent Picture*, when the sad news came that Bebe Daniels had passed away on Tuesday, March 16.

"The interview in this issue was recorded last summer, when Bebe looked so well, and we believed — and hoped — that she was on the road to recovery. Then on November 9, only days before Bebe had arranged with me to make a personal appearance at the National Film Theatre before a screening of *She's a Sheik*, she was readmitted into hospital. I wish somehow that she could have been present at that screening to see the immense enjoyment two packed houses — the programme had been sold out for weeks in advance — gained from her delightful performance in what, when all said and done, was nothing more than a typical twenties programme filler.

"Bebe is gone, but how many stars have left such a great legacy? How many stars can be said to have entertained three generations; as a silent star in the teens and twenties, as a musical comedy star in the thirties and early forties, and as Britain's most popular radio personality in the late forties and early fifties. She remained at all times modest, hard-working and ever-helpful. She helped and encouraged many young people on the road to stardom. Above all she entertained this country at a time when it was fighting for survival. Again Britain is fighting for survival — economic survival — but now there is no Bebe to cheer us."

Glenda Jackson wrote to me:

"We were away on holiday when we heard the news about Miss Daniels and both my husband and myself were stunned. That she had known ill-health for some time, we knew, but she was so much a part of our 'growing up', through her radio programmes, that it didn't seem possible. Would you convey our sincere condolences to Mr Lyon. Theirs was a partnership in both public and private life which was genuinely exemplary."

Following a letter I had written to Arthur Lowe on another subject, he replied:

"Your letter reached me after Bebe Daniels' death had already been announced and mourned. Mourned as the death of a childhood sweetheart. For that is what she was to so many of us who, as schoolboys, had been in love with her from the other side of a silver screen ... One of the most wondrous things about being successful is working with, or hearing from, and being accepted by people who were already famous when I was young and unimportant, and I pray that I shall never ever grow out of hero worship in an age when it is considered fashionable to tear down idols. Bebe was such an idol and she will always live on in our hearts."

18 Southwick Street no longer exists. They tore it down along with all the other houses on the street. Now instead of the tall, thin houses, there are modern flats. But to anyone who passes that spot and remembers the house with the blue door ... and pauses ... they will hear the echo of elated conversation and laughter. They will hear two American voices saying, "Come on in!" ... "Hi there!", and see in their mind's eye 'Welcome' on the mat.

AFTERMATH

There is no sad ending to this story. Bebe, least of all, would not have wanted anyone to be unhappy for her or for grief to take over where the bright path of her life ended. She is with her mother in a quiet and beautiful cemetery just outside London. After the interment service, Ben brought home a rose from his tribute to her of forty red roses, one for each year of their married life. He put the rose in a small vase on his desk, beside the last and lifelike photograph he and Bebe had taken together in the flat. The rose did not die; it became petrified. When I finally left Dolphin Square in May 1972, the rose was still there, perfect in every detail, except the stalk was wooden.

For a time Ben seemed to be inconsolable. The family and friends rallied round, insisting he went to their homes as often as possible. We made sure he was never left alone. And here I feel I must make special reference again to Lily Coyle, Bebe's masseuse. She lived above us in Dolphin Square. We would phone her very late to see if she was still up. If she was and, despite her medical work the next day, she would come down and talk with us into the small hours until Ben could no longer keep awake and he had to sleep. To this day, Lily Coyle recalls the nicknames Bebe gave her, 'Lily of Laguna' and 'Lily of the Valley'. Hers is not a famous name, but like doctors and nurses she epitomized the selflessness of the medical profession.

In May 1971, Barbara's baby boy was born in St Teresa's Hospital, Wimbledon. "I arranged to go there," said Barbara, "not only because it's a wonderful hospital but because, if mother had still been there, we could have been together." Later, Barbara said, "She was a marvellous mother. I miss her like mad — now since I've had the baby more than ever."

And Richard . . . After walking alone through the streets and looking again at those newspaper placards saying farewell to his mother, he returned home and said, "I suddenly feel torn apart."

By June, we had persuaded Ben to visit the States, to see his sisters and friends.

Ben said of Bebe, "She was not only my wife, she was my life." In using this line in her *Sunday Express* column, Anne Edwards wrote:

"Just for once amid the clamour of people who are getting divorced, or being married for the fourth time, or not being married at all because they don't believe in it, we hear a small voice contradicting them.

"Just for once amid the din of people shouting for a new law which allows them to divorce in two years, we hear one man saying of his wife, 'She gave me forty years of the greatest happiness a man ever had.' "

BEN'S FILMS –
SILENTS AND TALKIES

WARNER BROS.
1919 *Open Your Eyes*

VITAGRAPH
1921 *The Heart of Maryland*

WILLIAM FOX
1922 *The Custard Cup*

FIRST NATIONAL
1923 *Potash and Perlmutter*
Flaming Youth
1924 *Painted People*
The White Moth

M-G-M
1924 *Wine of Youth*

FAMOUS PLAYERS-LASKY
Lily of the Dust

PARAMOUNT
Wages of Virtue

FIRST NATIONAL
So Big
1925 *One Way Street*
The Necessary Evil

FIRST NATIONAL
Winds of Chance
The Pace That Thrills
The New Commandment
1926 *Bluebeard's Seven Wives*
The Reckless Lady
The Savage
The Great Deception
The Prince of Tempters
1927 *The Perfect Sap*
High Hat
The Tender Hour
Dance Magic
For The Love Of Mike

F.B.O.
1929 *Air Legion*

DEFU
Dancing Vienna

COLUMBIA
The Quitter
The Flying Marine

1930 **UNITED ARTISTS**
1930 *The Lummox*

RKO
Alias French Gertie
(with Bebe)

UNIVERSAL
What Men Want

RKO
Hell's Angels

WARNER BROS.
A Soldier's Plaything

FIRST NATIONAL
1931 *Hot Heiress*

TIFFANY
Aloha

WARNER BROS.
My Past (with Bebe)

FIRST NATIONAL
Misbehaving Ladies

UNITED ARTISTS
Indiscreet

WARNER BROS.
Bought
Night Nurse

FIRST NATIONAL
Compromised
Her Majesty Love

RKO
1932 *Lady With A Past*

COLUMBIA
Big Timer

FOX
Weekends Only

COLUMBIA
By Whose Hand?

FOX
Hat Check Girl

WORLD WIDE
The Crooked Circle

WARNER BROS.
1933 *Girle Missing*

UNITED ARTISTS
I Cover the Waterfront

M-G-M
The Women in His Life

WARDOUR
1934 *I Spy* (U.S. title:
The Morning After)

MASCOT
Crimson Romance

RKO
Lightning Strikes
Twice

1935

FOX
Beauty's Daughter
(U.K. title: *Navy Wife*)

REPUBLIC
'Frisco Waterfront

COLUMBIA
Together We Live

REPUBLIC
1936 *Dancing Feet*
Down To The Sea

DELA FILMS
1937 *Not Wanted On Voyage*
(with Bebe)

MORGAN FILMS
1938 *Mad About Money*
(U.S. title: *He Loved*
An Actress)

GRAFTON FILMS
1939 *I Killed The Count*

WARNER-BRITISH
Confidential Lady

GAINSBOROUGH
1941 *Hi Gang!*

WARNER-BRITISH
This Was Paris
1943 *The Dark Tower*

HAMMER
1953 *Life With The Lyons*
1954 *The Lyons in Paris*
And many more

Courtesy: Anthony Slide, Editor,
The Silent Picture

BEBE'S - FEATURE FILMS -
SILENTS AND TALKIES

PARAMOUNT
1919 *Male and Female*
Everywoman
1920 *Why Change Your Wife?*
The Dancing Fool
Sick Abed
The Fourteenth Man

REALART
Oh, Lady, Lady
You Never Can Tell

PARAMOUNT
1921 *The Affairs of Anatol*

REALART
Two Weeks With Pay
She Couldn't Help It
Ducks and Drakes
The March Hare
One Wild Week
The Speed Girl
1922 *Nancy From Nowhere*
A Game Chicken

PARAMOUNT
North of the Rio Grande
Nice people
Pink Gods
Singed Wings
1923 *The World's Applause*
Glimpses of the Moon
The Exciters
His Children's Children
Sinners In Heaven
1924 *Unguarded Women*
Heritage of the Desert
Monsieur Beaucaire
Dangerous Money
Argentine Love

PRINCIPAL
Daring Youth

PARAMOUNT
1925 *Miss Bluebeard*
The Crowded Hour
The Manicure Girl
Wild, Wild Susan
Lovers in Quarantine
The Splendid Crime
1926 *Miss Brewster's Millions*
Volcano
The Palm Beach Girl
The Campus Flirt
Stranded In Paris
1927 *A Kiss In A Taxi*
Senorita
Swim, Girl, Swim
1928 *She's A Sheik*
The Fifty-Fifty Girl
Hot News
Feel My Pulse
Take Me Home
What A Night!

RKO
1929 *Rio Rita*
1930 *Love Comes Along*
Alias French Gertie
   (with Ben)
Dixiana
Lawful Larceny

UNITED ARTISTS
1931 *Reaching For The Moon*

WARNERS
My Past (with Ben)
The Maltese Falcon
The Honor Of The Family

	WARNER BROS.		BRITISH ALLIANCE
1932	*Silver Dollar*	1936	*A Southern Maid*
1933	*42nd Street*		
			BRITISH LION
	COLUMBIA	1938	*Not Wanted On Voyage*
	Cocktail Hour		(with Ben)
	UNIVERSAL		WARNERS-TEDDINGTON
	Counsellor At Law	1939	*The Return of Carol Deane*
	BRITISH INTERNATIONAL COLUMBIA		GAINSBOROUGH
1934	*The Song You Gave Me*	1941	*Hi Gang!*
	WARNER BROS.		HAMMER
	Registered Nurse	1953	*Life With The Lyons*
		1954	*The Lyons In Paris*
	FOX		
1935	*Music Is Magic*		

BEBE AND BEN'S SONGS

What was old yesterday is new today . . . It is interesting to see how many of the songs Bebe and Ben sang over the years have become popular again in the '70s, like these which they sang together:

There's A Small Hotel
Three Little Fishes, who swam all over the dam . . . dam
Easter Parade
Little Sir Echo
Smile In The Morning, Up In The Morning
What A Swell Party This Is
You're The Tops
Jeepers Creepers
Let's Put Out The Lights And Go To Sleep
'Swonderful, 'Smarvellous, That You Should Care For Me
Little Lambs Eat Ivy
The Folks Who Live On The Hill
Who Stole My Heart Away?
It's Delightful, It's Delicious, It's D'Lovely
Love And Marriage

And a selection of Bebe's songs:
Rio Rita
Deep Purple
Smoke Gets In Your Eyes
South Of The Border, Down Mexico Way

42nd Street
You're Getting To Be A Habit With Me
Just One Of Those Things
Who Knows Where Or When?
The Best Things In Life Are Free
The Very Thought Of You
Let's Fall In Love
I Only Have Eyes For You
Night And Day
Deep In The Heart Of Texas
Merry Christmas To You
These Foolish Things
Just Like A Melody From Out Of The Sky
Who's Got The Last Laugh Now
Our Love Affair, Was Meant To Be
Is It True What They Say About Dixie?
When They Begin The Beguine
Room Five Hundred and Four
So In Love With You Am I
What Is This Thing Called Love?
I Get A Kick Out Of You
You'd Be So Nice To Come Home To
Umbrella Man — any umbrellas, any umbrellas to
    mend today
It Might As Well Be Spring
Body And Soul
Broadway Melody
When The Moon Shines Bright On Pretty Red Wing
It Had To Be You
If I Only Had Wings
On The Trail Of The Lonesome Pine
We're Going On A Summer Holiday
Yankee Doodle Went To Town, Riding on a Pony
We're In The Money
A Slow Boat To China
A Foggy Night In London Town
That Old Black Magic.